A PERSONAL JOURNEY

PORTRAIT OF A WOMAN AND JESUS

HE LOOKS THROUGH YOUR EYES AND INTO YOUR HEART

BY
BARBARA QUILLEN EGBERT

ARTWORK BY
WILSON ONG

Printed in the United States of America

Quillen Egbert, Barbara

Portrait of a Woman and Jesus — A Personal Journey
He Looks Through Your Eyes and into Your Heart

ISBN: 978-096617359-8
LCCN: 2011927657

Artwork: Wilson Ong
Cover and book design: John Egbert
Layout design: Cardinal Graphics and Design

Published by: New Voice Publications
PO Box 14133
Irvine, CA 92623

A PERSONAL JOURNEY

PORTRAIT OF A WOMAN AND JESUS

HE LOOKS THROUGH YOUR EYES AND INTO YOUR HEART

Dedicated to the reader (you!):

May Jesus use these words to bring wholeness and eternal restoration into your life.

ACKNOWLEDGEMENTS

This project called *Portrait of a Woman and Jesus* is built upon a foundation of prayers, encouragement, feedback and suggestions from family, friends and the talented people placed in my path to assist in completion. I am grateful for those who walked with me through the journey of writing and publication.

Portrait of a Woman and Jesus is all and only about the Son of God — Jesus — and written so every reader will have a deeper understanding of how much she is loved and valued by Him. Jesus has walked with me through every page of this project, and I humbly acknowledge the Holy Spirit's inspiration, counsel and guidance.

Words from those who have journeyed before you . . .

Portrait of a Woman and Jesus is a spiritual journey that takes the reader to a deep level of intimacy with Christ. The voice of Jesus is painted throughout the pages of this book, and it is very evident that the power of the Holy Spirit orchestrated the questions that the author presents. Those that travel the path of emotional healing will delight in this book! Their light and path will become visible as they share their fears and doubts face-to-face with Jesus. As the reader identifies with Christ through these writings and allows the Lord's restorative healing power to take place, the heart is motivated to follow the journey that has been divinely inspired.

— **Mary Larez**, Women's Small Group Prayer and Emotional Healing Leader

Beautiful, Poignant and Rich! Each portrait takes you right into Scripture and allows you to have a personal encounter with Jesus that is powerful, touching and moving! This study will inspire, strengthen and WOW your relationship to Jesus!

— **Michelle Woroniecki**, Core Leader, Women's Small Groups & Life Groups

Portrait of a Woman and Jesus, is a passionate and intimate look at how the King of kings values and empowers each woman to rise to who she was created to be. As you open the pages of this book and step inside, you will find that Jesus is drawing you to Himself with His "cords of love" to ask you with His still voice, "Beloved, how can I heal you?" I found myself in each of these women in such a relatable way that it chipped away at the hard crust I have allowed to self-protect my heart. I believe that if you invest yourself in these stories, you will hear Jesus asking you to step out in faith and see yourself not as the world does, but through His loving eyes.

— **Kathleen Rodarte**, Trainer, Women's Small Group Leaders

As a Marriage and Family Therapist, I was intrigued by the author's sensitivity to the women of the Bible. The portrayal of their circumstances is representative of their underlying feminine emotional structure. The questions at the end of each chapter were especially provocative. They brought to mind personal experiences from the past in a deep and meaningful way. I inquired of the author as to where she obtained so many insightful questions. She indicated that they just came to her. There is no doubt in my mind that God's Spirit is present in this book. It is a valuable resource for feminine life roles.

— **Winifred A. Gahm**, M.P.A., M.A., MFT

My friendship with Barbara Quillen Egbert began a few years ago, when we met at a Small Group Leader gathering. It wasn't until Barb spoke of her own portrait about meeting Jesus that I wanted to dive into her unedited, still forming manuscript. I was not to be disappointed. The portraits of each woman, along with the accompanying masterful paintings, touched me in ways I was not prepared. My prayers join Barb's as you open this book and step into this study. Ask the Lord what He would want to teach you, and prepare to be transformed from ordinary to extraordinary through the understanding of how deeply you are loved.

— **Wendy Hubbard**, Prayer Leadership, Women's Ministries, Eternal Friend and Fellow Pilgrim

A PERSONAL JOURNEY

PORTRAIT OF A WOMAN AND JESUS

HE LOOKS THROUGH YOUR EYES AND INTO YOUR HEART

PREFACE

Essence of this Personal Journey

This personal journey is written to complement the book *Portrait of a Woman and Jesus — He Looked Through Her Eyes and into Her Heart*. The reader will have an opportunity to observe the lives of women who were the beneficiaries of a brief, yet intimate encounter with Jesus. Though these encounters took place over two thousand years ago, we will see how many of the issues these Biblical women faced are similar to ours.

You will witness Jesus' intent and love for the women He encountered and transfer it to your own life, gaining a deeper awareness of Jesus' zealous love for you. Jesus desires to bring wholeness into all areas of your life — most importantly by spiritually reconciling you to your heavenly Father and giving you life, now and eternally. By reading about Jesus' responses to the various women in these portraits, you can gain confidence in His ability to bring physical restoration, emotional and relational redemption into your life as well.

With every portrait you will be encouraged to relate to the woman's situation and identify with her circumstances, needs and feelings. Each woman was deeply impacted by Jesus' spoken words of truth. She experienced one or more of the characteristics of God as Scripture was fulfilled in a personal way for her. What are some of the timeless lessons learned from Jesus' responses? Are you able to appreciate the effect Jesus had on each woman? How do His words of truth impact *you*?

As you put yourself into the sandals of the Biblical women Jesus encountered, I pray that you will grasp to a greater degree Jesus' desire to deepen His relationship with *you*! Out of His limitless love and ability to look through *your* eyes and into the depths of *your* heart, Jesus will interact with *you* on an intimately personal level. He will meet *your* unique needs and desires.

How do you respond when Jesus interacts with you? We will see how the women in these stories displayed joy, gratitude, praise and devotion. These enduring examples will encourage you to respond from your heart when Jesus impacts your life. Ultimately, you will want to say, as our sisters did so many years ago, "Come and see my Jesus! Let me tell you what He has done for me!"

> *But these are written so that you may believe Jesus is the Messiah, the Son of God, and by believing you may have life in His name.* John 20:31 HCSB

INTRODUCTION

The Heart of a Woman

To understand a woman, one must revisit the original intent and purpose for the feminine gender as expressed in the Bible. This overview will provide a background to understanding a women's unique emotional makeup and underscore Jesus' ability to relate to and address women — both as a gender class and as individuals.

Woman's Identity

Woman was originally created as the finishing touch of creation. She had infinite ***value*** because she was created in the image and likeness of God (Genesis 1:27) and without her, man was incomplete (Genesis 2:18). She was important and absolutely essential to accomplish the mission entrusted to humans.

What were the characteristics of the God-designed woman? How was she made in God's image and likeness?

She was ***beautiful***. Woman had captivating physical beauty and intriguing qualities of femininity that were different from "man." I imagine the first woman lived freely and fully from a pure and tender heart that was expressed through laughter, playful affection, curiosity and emotional sensitivity.

She was given a ***significant purpose***, shared equally with man in exploration, discovery and adventure and was destined to take on the irreplaceable role as life-giver, mother of all.

She was ***loved*** by God, cherished by her husband and created to freely give and receive affection.

She was ***relational***, as she enjoyed daily communion with her Creator and was emotionally and physically intimate with her husband.

She was ***secure*** and ***safe*** in her physical surroundings, enjoyed the freedom to explore and had sufficient daily food. She was confident in her relationship with God, basking in the revelation of her value, beauty and purpose. She felt affirmed in her relationship with her husband because she was treated with respect and highly esteemed as a partner in the human destiny.

Woman was complete — with all of her spiritual, physical and emotional needs met. She was fully alive, living life according to the will of her Creator. She radiated confidence and assurance of her status and potential. Life in the Garden was good — actually very good!

Therefore, since the beginning of time, a woman's identity revolves around the words ***value***, ***beauty***, ***significance***, ***love*** and ***security***. She is ***relational*** to the core of her being, created to enjoy a spiritual relationship with her Creator and designed to nurture relationships with family and friends.

How does this section on a *woman's identity* speak to you?

The Fall and Curse

With one act of disobedience by the first humans Adam and Eve, subsequent Fall and accompanying Curse (Genesis 3:14-19), everything changed. The first two humans were banished from the Garden. Life outside the original Garden of Eden was hell, as is any separation from God. Food, water, warmth, clothing and shelter were needed for survival and challenging to obtain. The woman no longer felt safe or secure. She experienced distance in relationships and felt loneliness, abandonment and the certainty of death (Genesis 3:19).

Woman's relationship with her Creator was altered. Instead of confidence and assurance, she felt guilt, shame and fear. She was no longer secure in her standing with God and would need restoration of the spiritual relationship she was intended to enjoy.

The relationship between man and woman, as a gender class, was also profoundly altered. The strength of a man that was intended to cherish, defend and protect was frequently used to take advantage of "woman." As spoken of in the Curse, man would "rule over" woman (Genesis 3:16). To varying degrees, she would be oppressed and treated as a second-class person, even to the point of being bought and sold as property. Many times, and often beginning from childhood, woman would find herself powerless, with no voice, controlled and denied access to educational and growth opportunities. In an ultimate perversion of God's intent, female babies would be aborted to such a degree that "female infanticide" would define the action. Some cultures would hide their women and deny them personal freedom and autonomy that men enjoy.

Woman's beauty became an object of lust and far too often she was sexually assaulted. As the weaker gender and a result of the Curse, she became overpowered, exploited, prostituted and abused physically and emotionally. As a result, woman mistrusted man and his intentions toward her and experienced insecurity. The intended partnership and unity of the sexes became a battleground!

Another part of the Curse stated that there would be hostility between the serpent (Satan) and the woman (Genesis 3:15). Every good thing that was intended from the beginning was now opposed. Joy, peace, unity and personal fulfillment were thwarted by Satan's attempts to increase a woman's doubt of God's loving intentions toward her.

Given this new reality, woman experienced incompleteness. Anything less than the original intent produced a deficit, a gap, a need — with a desire and longing to return to the created ideal. Therefore, she consciously or unconsciously became motivated to address any deficiencies (whether physical, emotional, relational, mental or spiritual) and return to her original identity associated with life in the Garden. She sought the answers to the fundamental questions in her life that pointed to her original intent, purpose and surroundings:

- Do I have value?
- Am I beautiful?
- Do I have a significant purpose?
- Am I loved?
- Do I feel safe?

 **In what ways have you experienced the *Fall* and subsequent *Curse*?**

LIVING BETWEEN THE GARDEN AND KINGDOM

As we have seen, the original intent for humans has not played out well. Though fallen and under a curse, humanity was given hope through the prophesied arrival of a Savior and the promise of redemption and reconciliation (Isaiah 7:14, 9:6, 61:1-2). But as humans living outside the Garden, we are faced with the difficult and complex task of meeting our daily needs and desires as we wait for eternal restoration in God's Kingdom. We continue to experience gaps from our original identity and intent as manifested in the Garden, though our needs and desires vary with our circumstances. The concept of ***"need"*** implies a necessity — such as food, water and shelter — whereas a ***"desire"*** represents a fundamental longing. Although desires have been characterized as being of lesser importance than needs, we each have specific desires that give meaning and enjoyment to our lives.

Even as we wait for full restoration in the Kingdom, we long to live life to the full — physically, emotionally, mentally, relationally and spiritually. Just as all humans have unique gifts, talents and traits, each of us are motivated by a set of needs and desires determined by personality, circumstances and stage of life.

In Psalm 103:5 the Lord is praised because He "satisfies our desires with good things." Proper desires reflect a longing for a taste of the goodness that was initially experienced in the Garden and may include the desire for adventure, achievement, mastery and challenge. One woman may desire to be surrounded by beauty, to engage in recreational activities or experience the outdoors. Another woman may desire to create, develop a talent, travel or have a close friend. By giving us "good things," it shows the Lord understands our hearts as we have communicated our desires with Him and He gives us glimpses back to the original intent of the Garden or forward to life in His Kingdom.

Can we live without complete satisfaction of these needs and desires? Because we live in a "fallen" world, humans have learned to survive and function when needs and desires are not met. A mother may sacrifice her need for food to ensure her children are fed first. A woman may postpone her desire for personal growth and devote time to aging parents. Although security is important for women, there have been numerous times throughout history when women risked their lives for a meaningful cause. These sacrifices do not negate the need or desire, merely the priority of it. There are many examples of people through the ages who have endured great suffering, their needs and desires seemingly unmet, because they maintained hope in the promise of eternity when life will be restored to a glorious new and perfect reality.

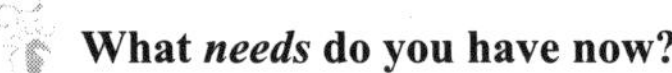

What *needs* do you have now?

What *desires* do you long for?

A Woman's Feminine Heart

A woman certainly has physical needs, but many of her needs and desires are not seen at face value. They are held in her heart. Throughout a woman's life she longs to have essential questions relating to her identity answered. The following questions relate to her original intent and purpose.

Do I Have Value? Value implies favorable regard for the importance, or worth, of the person. A woman has intrinsic desirability just because she, a creation of God, exists. Society places monetary value on people based on worldly standards. For many women, there is no monetary value placed on the mothering, care-giving and housekeeping roles they play, so it is common for women to question their value and suffer from low esteem.

Value also implies appreciation. It is common for a woman to ask (if not explicitly, then in her heart), "Am I appreciated? Am I wanted or needed?" If a woman has not received affirmation of her value from parents and significant persons in her life, she most likely will seek to fill that void of unfulfilled identity. She might believe that "other lovers" will somehow fill the emotional hole in her heart that is reserved only for heart-to-heart intimacy with Jesus. These "other lovers" may include pursuit of improper sexual relationships, abuse of food, alcohol, drugs, even busyness. Thankfully, even if a woman has not been validated by humans, the knowledge that God affirms her specialness can overcome the emptiness in her soul, angst in her heart and nagging question of worth.

What are your thoughts regarding your *value*?

Am I Beautiful? Because woman was created as the essence of beauty at creation, this question is central to her identity. The pursuit of the answer regarding her beauty will be a primary conscious or unconscious motivator throughout her life. Unfortunately, many are given the wrong impression that the pursuit of beauty is ungodly. Though God's viewpoint of beauty is different from cultural standards, He delights in validating a woman's beauty — not solely based on outward beauty that is valued by worldly standards, but beauty that also includes inner qualities.

What are your thoughts regarding your *beauty*?

Am I loved? A woman longs to be loved unconditionally — loved for her heart, presence, beauty, nurturing nature and life-giving goodness. She does not want to be loved conditionally — for what others can get from her, if she satisfies someone's expectations or even based on what she willingly gives. She wants to be cherished for who she uniquely is.

What are your thoughts regarding *being and feeling loved*?

Do I have a significant purpose? A woman desires to make a contribution of special consequence. A woman asks, "Do I (my unique person) matter? Is what I have to offer important and substantive? Do I have a purpose greater than myself? Do I contribute to a cause worth fighting for? What legacy am I leaving for the next generation?"

A woman desires to play a role in life that has transcendence — the awareness that she is part of a bigger story where her contributions are noble, worthy and significant. She wonders if she has a purpose beyond doing the mundane tasks commonly associated with women.

Unfortunately, society downplays the importance of the mothering and homemaking roles and many women suffer from a trivialized life of perceived insignificance. The care-giving role of mothering needs to be affirmed to communicate that mothers are needed and appreciated. They need to know that their contribution is of great worth, has special meaning and is making a significant difference, specifically in the life of a child.

Not all women are mothers, though, and many women pursue significance as they use their God-given gifts to benefit others. A woman desires to develop her talents and become the woman she was created to be. Her heart seeks confirmation that she plays a significant role as a person, as well as for how she is connected to others and is needed by them.

 **What are your thoughts regarding your *significance*?**

 **How do you view the significance of the *mothering role*?**

Am I safe? Women have a foundational need for security, literally to feel safe. Though this need will vary for women due to personal circumstances, women tend to have a greater physical and emotional need for security than men. In general, women are not as tall as men, have less muscle mass and are physically the "weaker" gender. Many women fear being taken advantage of, underscoring their personal need to trust others. A woman may experience varying levels of anxiety about being able to defend herself and is relieved emotionally when she is protected from physical harm.

The need for feeling safe is intensified when a woman lives alone, as when single, widowed or destitute, having no one to care for her, defend her, provide for her or to be her advocate. Because of a woman's awareness of her potential vulnerability, there can be accompanying fear, hesitation and loss of independence.

Though many women are financially independent and live in communities that provide relative physical safety, an emotional component to the need for security may still remain. Does a married woman feel secure that her husband is committed to her? Does she fear being abandoned?

 **What are your thoughts regarding *safety and security*?**

A woman is relational and desires intimacy with others. For most women, the longing for intimacy is primarily *emotional*, seeking a connection of heart and soul with another person. A woman seeks to establish relationships in which there are opportunities to share lives and hearts by giving love and support to others. When a woman trusts a relationship, she will allow herself to become vulnerable — to be honest and exposed to a person, sharing innermost thoughts, fears, dreams, grief, hurts and triumphs.

Because God created women as emotional beings, a woman feels the need to nurture, to mother, to give, serve, support, encourage and to love. Though many women directly nurture their children, women also find avenues to naturally nurture others by giving encouragement, becoming team players, affirming life and goodness and offering emotional support to family, friends and coworkers.

What are your thoughts regarding *emotional intimacy*?

Intimacy can include *affection*, though not primarily sexual intimacy. When a woman feels emotionally connected with her husband, *sexual intimacy* is a natural outcome. A woman wants to be reassured that she is loved, cherished and pursued — first and foremost, for her heart, not primarily for a sexual relationship.

What are your thoughts regarding *affection* and *sexual intimacy*?

A woman fundamentally experiences the need for *spiritual intimacy*. Most likely during every woman's life she will ask God, "Do You know me? Are You concerned about the issues on my heart? Can I trust You? Will You love me unconditionally?" Many women understand that though their human relationships are flawed or have failed, they are seeking the assurance of an intimate relationship with a perfect and unfailing God.

Intuitively, though maybe not acknowledged, we want to know God and yearn to know how He sees us through His eyes. A woman's life is changed when she knows she was created to have a relationship with her Creator — that she was created for His pleasure and His glory and that He can be trusted. Only because of His goodness and unconditional love is this possible.

What are your thoughts regarding *spiritual intimacy*?

Jesus Understood a Woman's Heart

As the Creator of all, Jesus perfectly understood the inner workings of a human's body, mind and heart, as well as His original intent for males and females. He alone had the capacity to look into the innermost part of a woman's heart and discern her needs and desires. Only Jesus had, and has, the ability to answer the central questions relating to a woman's identity: *Do I have value? Am I beautiful? Am I loved? Do I have a significant purpose? Am I safe?*

Jesus affirmed a woman's value. Jesus radically changed the perception of the value and worth of women by treating them with dignity, respect and as individuals of importance irrespective of their gender. His conduct toward women was in stark contrast to that which so many women have experienced. Throughout history, women have been devalued, subjected to subservient status and abused. Women have been treated as possessions and have been taken advantage of physically and emotionally. In some cultures women have been perceived to be second-class citizens and denied personal rights similar to men. Jesus' revolutionary acknowledgment and interaction with women had an immediate and timeless impact on society as a gender class and on women as individuals.

Jesus commonly interacted with a woman as an individual, independent of the other roles she may have been playing. He did not work through a woman's husband or her father, but directly with *her*. On several occasions Jesus' encounter with a woman did relate to her role as a mother or widow. But His response, whether with personal healing or healing for her child, was given as a direct reflection of the desire of *her* unique heart. Each woman was valued for who she was as a person, with her own identity, and Jesus responded to her needs or desires in a *personal* way.

Jesus valued emotional expression and demonstrated that a woman's heart responds to unconditional love. Jesus understood that at the core of a woman's heart is a longing to be loved for who she is as a uniquely created person. He did not trivialize or minimize her emotions and was comfortable when a woman tearfully shared the depths of her heart. He even seemed to encourage her emotional vulnerability by listening to her and honoring her requests while quieting any objections by observers.

Jesus did not condemn. Jesus loved a woman regardless of her human failings, sins and history of mistakes. Though never condoning a life outside the eternal will of the Father, neither did He condemn. Jesus did, however, influence those around Him to a higher calling of eternal perspective, continuing to show unfailing love when humans stumbled.

Jesus gave significance to women through recognition of their role as participants in His ministry, even allowing them to travel at times with His "ministry team." Women supported Him financially and many women stood courageously by Jesus at the cross (Matthew 27:55-56). The significance Jesus gave to women was underscored by the fact that He revealed Himself as the risen Christ first to a woman. Jesus also affirmed the timeless values of trust, faithfulness, belief and compassion that women exhibited. Though many of these women were unnamed in the Bible and without social status, He used their humanly insignificant lives as examples of eternal worth.

Jesus provided the ultimate security. Jesus was concerned when a woman was not provided for, and especially for the plight of widows. Because He understood a woman's need to feel secure physically, emotionally and spiritually, His encounters with those who needed security resulted in a sense of emotional comfort and safety. Through Jesus' death and resurrection, He provided the ultimate security. Many women sensed that though poor, destitute or devalued in the eyes of society, they were eternally safe and confidently waited for their place in Jesus' Kingdom.

Jesus loved unconditionally by grace. He loves you too, unconditionally, not because of what you can offer and give to Him, but because He loves and values you for *who you are*. Jesus places you in high esteem — regardless of the level of worth society may ascribe to you. He paid the price for your redemption with the ultimate sacrifice of His life, bestowing on you value, worth and regard. Remember that you are *His* Creation! That is the spiritual foundation you are assured of and upon which you can build.

Jesus came to save, restore and give life. As Creator, it certainly was not Jesus' intent for a woman to be abused, suffer, be alone, feel insecure, worthless or insignificant. But because she, along with the human race, had fallen from the original intent, Jesus would fill other relational roles in her life — Savior, Redeemer, Friend, Defender, Protector and Bridegroom.

Jesus was sent to earth by His and our heavenly Father so that you could have life to the full and live in freedom through an intimate relationship with Him. Because Jesus came to earth in human form, He relates to your humanity and meets your individual needs in a way that speaks to your unique circumstances and heart. He alone can provide for your physical, emotional and spiritual needs. Only He understands you personally and has the ability and power to restore and complete you.

Jesus is the same — yesterday, today and forever (Hebrews 13:8). You can be assured that the way Jesus encountered, interacted with and responded to women when He walked the earth is the same as He has the desire and power to do today! You can trust that the relationship Jesus had with the Biblical women is the same that He makes possible for you today.

Before we get started: What thoughts do you have regarding your relationship with Jesus? What specific issues in your life do you desire to be resolved? Do you have any questions you would like to address? *(You may find it helpful to write those ideas down so that as you progress through the chapters, you will be aware of how those issues are addressed.)*

MY PRAYER FOR YOU

Jesus, I trust that because of Your good and perfect nature, You will reveal yourself to this dear woman in a dramatic way. Only You can see into the depths of this woman's heart and have the desire and power to complete and release her to fulfill the potential You have created for her. Please help her to believe You are joyfully walking beside her through this journey because she is precious to You. I pray expectantly in Your name, Amen!

Portrait Of An Encounter With Jesus

We are ready to journey through thirteen portraits of an encounter with Jesus. Each portrait includes text from the book *Portrait of a Woman and Jesus*, has space to record your thoughts and is arranged by the following section headings.

In Her Shoes

The first section of each portrait revisits the book's description of "the scene" — imagining the face-to-face encounter a woman had with Jesus. The central question asked is, "How do you identify with the woman and her story?"

Face-To-Face With Jesus

Only Jesus has the divine ability to look into the human heart and know our deepest thoughts, doubts and fears. In the second section of each portrait, we will explore the question, "What did Jesus see when He looked into her heart?"

> *But Jesus knew what was in their hearts, and he would not let them have power over him. No one had to tell him what people were like. He alreadt knew them.* John 2:24-25 CEV

> *For the LORD searches every heart and understands the intention of every thought.* 1 Chronicles 28:9 HCSB

> *The LORD does not look at the things people look at. People look at the outward appearance, but the LORD looks at the heart.* 1 Samuel 16:7 NIV

> *For You alone know the human heart.* 2 Chronicles 6:30 HCSB

> *The LORD looks at the world from his throne in heaven, and he watches us all. The LORD gave us each a mind, and nothing we do can be hidden from him.* Psalm 33:13-15 CEV

This section of the workbook includes verses primarily from The Psalms. King David, the main psalmist, boldly recorded his heartfelt, authentic, transparent and honest feelings. David was not afraid to express his innermost thoughts to God, though he typically ended a psalm by praising the Lord, keeping an eternal perspective and remembering that "God is God — and we are not."

Just as Eve was deceived by a lie from Satan, we can be deceived by lies. Satan plants seeds of doubt regarding God's goodness and intentions toward us. Is God trustworthy? Is He withholding good from me? Does He really care? The central question to this section is: "What does Jesus see when He looks into your heart?"

Words Spoken To The Heart

On numerous occasions, Jesus said, ***"I tell you the truth."*** The third section focuses on the brief phrase of truth spoken by Jesus which addressed the central issue in the woman's life. These words of truth spoke to issues of who He is, how He viewed the woman and how He responded to the woman's need.

Though our emotional feelings are real, they may not tell the entire story, give a complete picture from an eternal perspective or always reflect truth. With Jesus' words, God's perspective, we are set free from human doubts and lies told by Satan, the father of lies (John 8:44).

So Jesus said to the Jews who had believed Him, ***"If you continue in My word, you really are My disciples. You will know the truth, and the truth will set you free."*** John 8:31-32 HCSB

Adam and Eve originally based their identity and relationship with God, but turned from God after doubting Him. They exercised their free will by using human reasoning and then chose to reject and disobey God. Since that first act of rebellion against God, *all* humans have continued in that pattern of sinfulness, falling woefully short of God's glory (Romans 3:23).

Jesus gives us an opportunity to return to God — to turn back again to our original and intended identity and relationship with God. Many of His words of truth speak of some form of restoration — physically, emotionally or in context of the woman's spiritual relationship. Only Jesus has the ability to make *all* things eternally new through redemption, restoration and transformation.

Scripture in this section primarily includes quotes from Jesus. Let His words of truth bring healing, life and freedom to your heart and soul!

"So if the Son sets you free, you will be free indeed." John 8:36 NIV

An Encounter With Jesus

How did Jesus' words of truth impact the woman He encountered? How do His words of truth transform *your* life? We will see how truth dispels lies, gives hope for complete and eternal restoration and speaks of God's faithful love and intentions toward *you*.

I heard God say two things: "I am powerful, and I am very kind." Psalm 62:11-12 CEV

In this fourth section we will explore how an encounter with Jesus impacts *you*. As with the women He encountered, I trust you will be encouraged to share *your* stories of God's goodness with others.

Your Encounter With Jesus

Space is provided to write what you sense Jesus revealed relative to your journey through the portrait.

My Prayer For You

I have written a prayer for you at the end of each portrait and hope you will be blessed to know that you have been prayed over during each step of this journey. I am confident God will honor my prayers on your behalf, believing that He is powerful and very kind.

Your Prayer

Space is included at the end of each portrait to write a prayer that was inspired by your journey. If you are unsure of what to pray, rewrite my prayer and personalize it by inserting your name. Pray slowly and intentionally, allowing each phrase and sentence to move deeply within your heart.

Final Thoughts Before Your Journey Begins

This journey, though personal, can also be experienced within a small group setting. To derive the full and intended benefit of this journey (whether done individually or simultaneously within the context of a small group), I highly recommend the reader take the time to prayerfully and courageously read ALL the text, questions and scriptures. The questions may or may not be applicable for your situation, so concentrate on the ones that address the deep issues in your heart. If there are questions that are painful to answer, I encourage you to surrender your fears and doubts and remain committed to the journey, relying on Jesus to guide you through the process of restoration.

It is important to meditate on each scriptural passage, allowing the words of truth to settle into your heart. Ask God to use Scripture to reveal and heal any lies, hurts or doubts about Him.

For Group Leaders: The dynamics of your group — time commitment, size and individual circumstances of the members — will determine if it would be best to spend one or two weeks on each portrait. Regardless of the pace with which you proceed, encourage your women to individually journey through the assigned chapter *prior to* your group meeting. Challenge the ladies to take the time to courageously answer the questions, thoughtfully read the scriptures and allow the words of truth to speak directly into their hearts. As the leader during a group discussion, it might be helpful to select one question out of each section to focus on or ask each woman to share the question and verse that spoke most intimately to her heart. And pray, pray, pray for God's restoring and healing presence to walk with your ladies each step of this journey toward wholeness in Him.

My Prayer For You

Jesus, as the reader embarks on this journey, I ask that You help her see and know You more clearly. Gently answer the questions she has about You and Your goodness toward her. Show her the incomprehensible worth she has in Your eyes! Please give her courage and help her to feel safe when entrusting her heart to Your healing touch. Let her know Your undeniable desire and ability to bring restoration and wholeness into her life. Bless her with such overwhelming conviction of Your reality that she is compelled to tell others how she has experienced Your unconditional love. In Your name I pray, Amen!

Your Thoughts Or Prayer As You Begin This Journey

The Woman Who Touched Jesus

Matthew 9:20-22, Mark 5:24-34, Luke 8:42-48

The miracle of birth demonstrates the undeniable power and beauty of a Creator. When looking into the face of a newborn, we are reminded of the precious gift of life and how each individual is uniquely made in the image of God. Yet, we are also aware that each life-sustaining breath temporarily suspends our ultimate human reality — a return to dust of the earth from which we were made (Genesis 3:19).

Your Faith Has Healed You.

Throughout the course of life, our humanness brings an assortment of aches and pains, scraped knees, tooth decay, graying hair, headaches, sprained ligaments, broken bones and vision loss. Many individuals suffer from severe health issues genetically predisposed at birth, accumulated from lifestyle choices or caused by an accident. Though originally created for eternity, we live in temporary and fragile shells.

In this first portrait, we are introduced to a woman who lived with the reality of her humanity and faced daily challenges because of a chronic health issue. Though she sought relief from the sources available to her, she knew that her only hope for complete restoration was in Jesus. Her example of faith, and Jesus' subsequent response to one anonymous woman in the crowd, encourages us to continue in our trusting pursuit of Jesus, no matter how long the wait might be.

In Her Shoes

Clutching the shawl tightly around her head, a woman discretely made her way through the crowd, avoiding eye contact with anyone she might have known. Why did she want to go unnoticed? She had been suffering the indignity and embarrassment of chronic bleeding for twelve years!

Every disability or disease brings a particular set of challenges and heartbreak. But a woman with a hemorrhage was probably impacted more severely than if she had a different ailment. According to Jewish law, when a woman bleeds from the womb she is considered "unclean." Everything and anyone she touches during her time of bleeding is infected with uncleanness as well.

Imagine this woman's despair after suffering for twelve years! She was probably shunned and ostracized. She lived an isolated social life of humiliation, not allowed to worship or have a natural friendship with others. Not only did bleeding cause a major inconvenience, it also affected her entire health. She suffered from chronic low physical energy and possibly from anemia.

This woman may have been single, potentially dooming her to poverty and loneliness. If she were married, there must have been considerable strain on her relationship. Most likely she was unable to have children. In a society that equated a woman's worth with the ability to produce children, this hemorrhaging could have had accompanying emotional feelings of uselessness, as well as deep depression.

Placing her hope in doctors was futile. They had provided no answers, but depleted her financial resources in her quest for healing. Her physical situation worsened and her anguish reached the desperation point. She overheard stories of a man named Jesus who had healing power and was in town. He was her last and only hope!

Though it was a risk to be seen publicly or to touch anyone, she was compelled to search for Jesus. She must find Him! Maybe He will heal me, she thought. She was hopeful that the number of people hurrying to see Him would aid her desire for obscurity. She felt so insignificant and worthless, not wanting to bother Him. She did not pursue a spoken word or even a visual acknowledgement from Him. Instead, she determined to inconspicuously touch His clothes, believing that He had the power to restore her health and make her "clean."

That must be Jesus! Inching her way through the crowd she boldly moved right behind Him, reached out and gently touched His garment. Instantly, she sensed that her bleeding has stopped and reflexively gasped as she felt strength and wholeness wash over her body for the first time in twelve years! Barely grasping the reality of the miracle, she was jolted by Jesus' reaction.

He immediately turned around and asked, "Who touched Me?" because He knew healing power had gone out from Him. Instead of walking away and letting her experience the miracle privately, Jesus set up an encounter that would provide a witness to the crowd.

Jesus continued to pursue the issue of who had touched Him, looking around at those surrounding Him. However, all were denying it. Though the woman tried to avoid His searching look, their eyes met and she could no longer go unnoticed. She fell at His feet, trembling with fear as she told Him the whole truth.

How do you relate to this woman?

Can you understand her desperation? Do you currently feel depressed? Despondent? Fearful? Maybe even hopeless?

Do you identify with this woman because of a previous healing?

Do you know a woman who has suffered for numerous years?

Does she continue to have hope while enduring her suffering? How does she remain hopeful?

Are *you* currently experiencing a physical trial?

How has an emotional trial left you feeling beleaguered, exhausted or brokenhearted?

Instead of a bleeding womb, do you have a wounded and bleeding heart that you desire to be healed?

How would you describe *your* trust in Jesus' ability to answer your prayers?

Have you ever "sought out" Jesus with the tenacity of this woman? If so, describe your faith experience.

Do you truly believe that Jesus is *your* last, most secure and only hope?

Do you believe in His power to heal and have faith to seek Him out and reach for Him?

Face-To-Face With Jesus

Why would Jesus be looking into eyes filled with fear? Maybe this woman felt guilty to have touched Him in her "unclean" state. Or maybe she felt she would be met with a rebuke for seeking Him in a secretive manner. Perhaps she feared the repercussions when it was discovered that she had broken a religious requirement. But instead of rebuke or anger, Jesus extended His hand in a reassuring gesture and listened as she told her story.

She shared the deepest part of her heart — the pain, suffering, embarrassment and rejection that she had endured for years! She also confessed why she had sought Him out anonymously and confirmed that she had been instantly healed. This ultimately became a public declaration of her faithful heart and Jesus' healing power.

By confronting this woman face-to-face, Jesus gave those present an opportunity to hear her story and to witness His loving response. Though Jesus was on His way to attend to the ill daughter of a prominent synagogue official, He graciously took the time to address an ordinary woman's undeniable need. By acknowledging this woman, *merely one woman in the crowd*, Jesus demonstrated that each individual matters.

Can you empathize with what Jesus sees when He looks into this woman's heart?

Can you relate to her "fear"? If so, describe how.

Are you afraid of seeking Jesus? Do you fear that you're not "good enough" or that you might not approach Him in the correct way?

Are you afraid to stand face-to-face with Jesus? Why?

Have you been taught that you don't have access to Jesus — that you can only approach Him through a religious ritual or religious leader?

Do not be far from me, because distress is near and there is no one to help. Psalm 22:11 HCSB

What are the deep and honest thoughts in your heart that Jesus alone can see?

Why would God be concerned with my issue?
I doubt that God can heal me.
God, do you care about me?
I don't want to bother Him.
I don't think God will come through for me.
Why did God make me like this?
God is too busy to listen to me.
I believe God can heal, but doubt that He will.
Miracles only happen to others.
My situation is hopeless.
Things don't work out for me.

If you have harbored these kinds of thoughts in your heart, you're not alone. Meditate on what the psalmist writes:

I am your servant! How long must I suffer? Psalm 119:84 CEV

What area in your life would you like to bring to Jesus to heal?

Are you seeking a physical healing?

In what way is your heart wounded, scarred, broken — maybe even bleeding, draining your life away?

Do you live in an isolated prison of "bleeding" that no one seems to see or understand?

Is there an emotional hurt inflicted by another that you are carrying? Are you having difficulty resolving that hurt? Why?

What burden, oppression or bondage in your life do you want to be freed from?

Do you feel free to come to Jesus and tell Him everything — laying all of your troubles, trials, worries, fears and hurts at His feet?

He heals the brokenhearted and binds up their wounds. Psalm 147:3 NIV

Can you visualize reaching out to Jesus, touching Him and seeking His response?

Are you avoiding Jesus' glance?

Do you feel unclean or unworthy to ask for His involvement in your life?

Have you reached the point where you want to trust Jesus, but are afraid to? What is your fear?

Have you been disappointed in the past with God and doubt His intentions towards you?

Please answer my prayer. I am completely helpless. Psalm 142:5 CEV

Are there parts of your heart that you are resistant to expose to Jesus? What might be standing in your way of total trust?

Have you been hurt by parents, friends, a pastor or religion and use that as an excuse *not* to pursue God? Can you admit the "who" or "what" that keeps you from moving forward toward God?

Have you lost faith in Jesus' power to heal because you feel that your prayers for restoration have gone unanswered?

Do you doubt that He will respond to your request now?

Is that what you would like to ask Jesus to heal — your doubt?

You are the one who put me together inside my mother's body, and I praise you because of the wonderful way you created me. Everything you do is marvelous! Of this I have no doubt. Nothing about me is hidden from you! I was secretly woven together deep in the earth below, but with your own eyes you saw my body being formed. Even before I was born, you had written in your book everything I would do. Psalm 139:13-16 CEV

How does the phrase *"merely one woman in the crowd"* speak to your heart?

Do you understand God's willingness to search YOU out, even in the crowd, to meet *your* needs?

Do you believe that He is seeking *you* out and that He is not too busy to respond to *you*?

You have looked deep into my heart, Lord, and you know all about me. You know when I am resting or when I am working, and from heaven you discover my thoughts. You notice everything I do and everywhere I go. Before I even speak a word, you know what I will say, and with your powerful arm you protect me from every side. I can't understand all of this! Such wonderful knowledge is far above me. Psalm 139:1-6 CEV

What would you like to say face-to-face to Jesus? (If you are afraid to speak from your heart, be assured that Jesus is gentle and kind. Have courage, dear daughter of His.)

Words Spoken To The Heart

After listening to her story, maybe spoken with a trembling voice as tears ran down her cheeks, He responded with words that elevated her humble status to one of favor, calling her "daughter," indicating her restoration to full identity in the community. He revealed to the crowd that her example of faith had healed her and she was now freed from suffering. He also calmed her fears by telling her to "go in peace."

What a response! An instant healing! Jesus gave the cure that she had sought in vain from doctors for *twelve years*. Not only was she healed physically, but Jesus also publicly restored her reputation in a profound way. Formerly perceived as "unclean," she received words of favor in front of the crowd she had previously avoided.

Instead of treating her with disdain, Jesus' interaction was done out of kindness and understanding. While initially it may have seemed harsh to force the issue of determining who had touched His robe, it was only through the immediacy of the healing touch and outpouring of her heart that the encounter could have the greatest impact on those who were gathered around. With a joyful smile, He released her from suffering and gave her peace. Jesus was her Healer, Savior and Redeemer. She had directly received His restoring power from just one touch.

"Take heart, daughter, your faith has healed you. Go in peace and be freed from your suffering." Matthew 9:22, Mark 5:34 NIV

How did these words from Jesus affect and/or change this woman?

What is your reaction to this example of kindness Jesus extended to this woman?

How do the following words from Jesus speak to *your* heart? Do they speak of Jesus' love for *you*?

"Are not five sparrows sold for two pennies? Yet not one of them is forgotten by God. Indeed, the very hairs of your head are all numbered. Don't be afraid; you are worth more than many sparrows." Luke 12:6-7 NIV

In what way does your heart ache for healing and restoration?

Are you seeking restoration of physical health?

Restoration of strained relationships?

Restoration of financial stability?

Restoration of reputation?

Restoration of trust, of hope?

Restoration in other areas?

"Don't be afraid; just believe." Mark 5:36 NIV

"But if you can do anything, take pity on us and help us." "'If you can'?" said Jesus. *"Everything is possible for him who believes." Immediately the boy's father exclaimed, "I do believe; help me overcome my unbelief!"* Mark 9:22-24 NIV

Do you sincerely believe Jesus has the *power* to heal and restore?

Do you trust in His ability to heal and restore?

Do you sincerely believe Jesus has the *desire* to heal and deliver you? Do you have faith that He is willing?

Does this story increase your faith by showing that Jesus desires to restore *you* and bring wholeness into *your* life?

Do you sincerely believe and trust Jesus has the *power* AND *desire* to heal and restore YOU?

Why does God desire your wholeness?

"What do you want me to do for you?" "Lord, I want to see, he replied." Luke 18:41 NIV

"Lord, if You are willing, You can make me clean." Reaching out His hand He touched him, saying, "I am willing; be made clean." Matthew 8:2-3 HCSB

Though this woman was blessed with a miraculous healing, we need to be reminded that God does not promise to always heal, deliver and restore, nor is He obligated to intervene in our lives. Not all requests for physical restoration are answered as we want or in the way we expect. But we all have hope for the promise of eternal restoration when our bodies, though weakened, will be renewed. Jesus provides courage and comfort to endure our trials while we faithfully wait for the time when we will be whole again. And if He chooses to heal because of reasons only understood by Him, we should be grateful for His gift of grace.

Have you considered that though suffering physically (prayers for healing apparently unanswered), other significant miracles or intervention could be taking place?

How is that possible?

Can you visualize reaching out to touch Jesus and trusting in His ability to know and provide exactly what you need?

Can you praise and thank Him for what you believe He can and will do, regardless of the outcome?

"Your Father knows what you need before you ask." Matthew 6:8 CEV

Knowing that Jesus is perfectly aware of your situation, what would you like to ask Him?

An Encounter With Jesus

This woman's life would never be the same after she touched Jesus' clothes. Jesus restored her health and standing in society's eyes, freeing her from years of hopelessness. Gone was the shame, replaced by confirmation that she was loved and valued in Jesus' eyes. He took the time to listen to her heart and responded completely to her need and desire to be healed.

Freedom from suffering! Physically she would be able to function normally as a woman again. If single, would she be able to pursue marriage? Would she be able to have children now? No longer was life dictated by the limitations of a physical ailment. Now she was able to move forward with plans for her life.

We can only imagine the emotional freedom that she would also experience. Freedom from shame, from withdrawal! She had renewed hope for her future and was able to enjoy relationships again because she was now considered "clean." Formerly ostracized, she would be socially accepted and could hold in her heart the words of special favor spoken by Jesus. What a contrast to live with joy instead of suffering and with dignity instead of shame.

What was it like to actually touch Jesus' garment and suddenly feel the healing power of restoration? What a story she had to share with others! Would she now walk with a smile on her face and with thankfulness and praise in her heart for the One she had directly encountered? Did she touch others with similar mercy and grace she was given?

Though this woman reached out to Jesus, it was her faith in Him that brought healing. We are not in proximity to Jesus as she was, but faith in His power still heals and restores. He knows your needs! Be encouraged to approach Jesus with confidence and boldness, trusting in His eternal goodness towards you.

Eventually this woman died. Jesus' power will restore her again — to a new and eternal life, where suffering and death cannot exist.

How did this woman experience God?

Have you experienced God in a similar way? Briefly summarize a story you share with others concerning God's hand on your life.

How has this woman's story given you hope and bolstered your faith in Jesus' desire and ability to heal and restore?

Do you believe Jesus will do the same for *you*?

As you see the desire of Jesus to restore, how does this encourage you to intensely seek healing and restoration in *all* areas of your life, including within your relationships?

I call to God Most High, to God who fulfills [His purpose] for me. Psalm 57:2 HCSB

Do you trust God to give you strength to face all of life's circumstances, knowing that in *His* timing, restoration will come?

Are you prepared to accept the fact that *His* timing may not be the same as yours?

Does this story give you courage to remain hopeful for *your* time of restoration and wholeness?

How is having "hope" a choice?

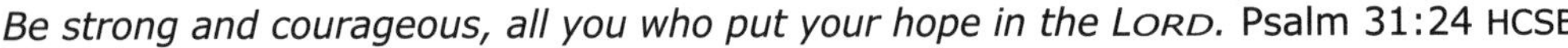

Be strong and courageous, all you who put your hope in the Lord. Psalm 31:24 HCSB

Are you willing to wait for restoration and wholeness, according to God's plan and purpose for your life?

What will you do while you wait for Jesus' healing touch?

Guide me in your truth and teach me, for you are God my Savior, and my hope is in you all day long. Psalm 25:5 NIV

How can God use you to bring His intense and loving desire for healing and wholeness to others?

How can you give the comfort and hope for eternal restoration to others?

You make our hearts glad because we trust you, the only God. Psalm 33:21 CEV

The Lord values those who fear Him, those who put their hope in His faithful love. Psalm 147:11 HCSB

Do you reflexively give glory to God after your prayers are answered, and even while you "wait"? If not, are you encouraged to do so beginning today?

One generation will declare Your works to the next and will proclaim Your mighty acts. I will speak of Your glorious splendor and Your wonderful works. They will proclaim the power of Your awe-inspiring works, and I will declare Your greatness. Psalm 145:4-6 HCSB

YOUR ENCOUNTER WITH JESUS

Jesus, what are You trying to teach me through this trusting woman's example? Write what you are hearing Him say to you.

Have you heard Him say, **"Your faith has healed you"**?

MY PRAYER FOR YOU

Lord, please reveal Yourself to this dear woman as a concerned heavenly Father who yearns to have a relationship with her. Though she is merely one woman in a crowd, show her Your willingness to take time to respond to her needs and cares. Demonstrate Your power to heal and restore all the areas in her life and heart she is entrusting to You. Calm her fears and let her know how much You love her, understand her and desire to free her from suffering. Lord, give her freedom and peace, so that she may give glory to You. Grow her faith as she relies on Jesus as her only hope. Use this woman to seek out those who are suffering and inspire her to speak Your words of compassion, restoration and hope to them. In Jesus' name, I pray. Amen!

YOUR PRAYER

Thoughts Regarding Your Journey Experience

A Grieving Mother

Luke 7:11-17

Due to a critical decision made by the first humans in the Garden of Eden, each of us will suffer loss in various forms throughout our lives — whether loss of a relationship, a dream, a cherished phase of life, innocence, hope, or even a pet. Because of our humanity, it is a certainty that we will witness the death a loved one, experience the depth of sorrow and be faced with how to cope with our loss. Though our grief seems inconsolable, we long for reassurance during these times.

Don't Cry.

In this portrait we are introduced to a woman who has been tragically acquainted with loss and insecurity. As bystanders, we are given a glimpse into the kindness, redemption and restoration given to her because of the empathetic heart of Jesus. He was acutely aware of this woman's need for comfort, protection and stability after a devastating life event, and His actions confirmed His foundationally good and loving heart.

In Her Shoes

The funeral procession with accompanying sounds of weeping and wailing was impossible to ignore. As Jesus and those traveling with Him were approaching the entrance to the city, their smiles and friendly conversations began to subside. It soon became clear that a large crowd from the town was escorting a woman and the body of her dead son to the burial grounds. They respectfully stepped aside to let the grieving procession pass.

We are not given specific details on the status of this woman, the age of her son or how he died. We do know that he was her only son and she was a widow. Many neighbors supported her through this tragic time, surrounding her with comforting arms. With the loss of her husband, and now her only son, this woman's situation looked hopeless and her audible mourning expressed the depth of her grief.

It only took one look for Jesus' heart to be touched by the double tragedy this woman was experiencing, and He stepped toward the open coffin. Those carrying the lifeless body hesitated and then stopped, sensing the presence of a man with authority. Confused, the downcast woman looked up at the man standing in front of her.

How do you relate to the grieving heart of this woman — as a mother, a widow or a friend to one who grieves?

Have you suffered an overwhelming grief? Explain how it was similar or dissimilar to this woman's situation.

Have you grieved because of the loss of *your* child?

Has there been a time when you have watched someone close to you grieve? Describe how their situation affected you.

If you are *not* a mother, is this a difficult story to read and relate to?

Have you been acquainted with sorrow because you desired to have a child, but were unable to?

Face-To-Face With Jesus

As Jesus looked through her eyes, He perceived a heart aching from profound grief. First she lost her husband and became a widow, and now she lost her only son. She had nothing left. Perhaps she feared what her future would now bring. Maybe she lost all will to continue on. Jesus could see into the depths of her anguish and hopelessness.

In her culture, a widow without a man to provide for her needs would likely become destitute, as she probably would be unable to earn a living for herself. Jesus would have been aware of the vulnerability of her impending poverty from losing her husband and son. Not only would the physical challenge of survival be severe, but the emotional outcome of her double loss was devastating. His heart went out to her, motivating Him to rescue her from the seemingly inevitable pit of loneliness that she now faced.

Maybe Jesus projected forward to the time when His own widowed mother would be grieving in a similar way for the loss of *her* son — an event that only He could foresee. His heart overflowed with empathy.

Describe a time of loss in your life and how it impacted you. How did you react to and deal with the loss?

Is your heart still grieving a loss?

Have you ever suffered so much loss that you did not want to continue living?

Are there unresolved issues in your life that cause angst and sorrow? Maybe your tears come from shattered dreams, dashed hopes, unfulfilled expectations or broken relationships.

Could you be grieving from mistakes made and the consequences of wrong choices? How does blame play a role in your grief?

Could it be that you have no more tears to shed because you are emotionally spent?

Is it possible that you have stuffed a hurt so deep within your heart that you are barely aware of it?

Can you identify the hurt that needs to be revealed and brought to Jesus' attention? Explain how you might be afraid to revisit or address the pain.

I am weary from my groaning; with my tears I dampen my pillow and drench my bed every night. My eyes are swollen from grief. Psalm 6:6-7 HCSB

When Jesus looks into your heart does He see sorrow or hurt, maybe even bitterness?

Might He see feelings of being overwhelmed or the fear of facing a seemingly insurmountable obstacle?

Have you ever found yourself in a place of instability, feeling a complete loss of control over your circumstances? If so, how?

Do you live with a feeling of insecurity and fear?

Do you feel heightened weakness and anxiety because of your fears? Explain your need for protection, to feel safe or secure.

I am worn out and weak, moaning and in distress. Psalm 38:8 CEV

Have any of these phrases ever surfaced in your thoughts?

I'm all on my own.
What difference does it make?
I'll have to figure it out myself.
God, why are You silent?
No one cares about me.
I am so scared.
What will become of me now?
It's so hard to keep going.
My life is over.
Why can't I seem to get over this?
How am I supposed to go on?
Will I ever recover from this hurt?
I don't want to die alone.
Life has no meaning anymore.
God, why did You cause this to happen to me?
I'm vulnerable to being hurt, so I must protect myself.

If you relate to any of the above phrases, can you explain why you feel the way you do?

Do you feel that God understands your situation?

Or do you feel "ignored" and doubt God's ability to personally interact with you?

My eyes grow weary [looking] for what You have promised; I ask, "When will You comfort me?" Psalm 119:82 HCSB

My God, my God, why have you deserted me? Why are you so far away? Won't you listen to my groans and come to my rescue? I cry out day and night, but you don't answer, and I can never rest. Psalm 22:1-2 CEV

Have you actively sought comfort from God during a grieving process?

Or did He just show up, reassure and rescue you like He did with this woman?

Are you confident that Jesus knows and understands your situation, cares for you and has the power to keep you safe and help you heal?

May Your faithful love comfort me, as You promised Your servant. Psalm 119:76 HCSB

What loss or hurt are you willing to entrust to Jesus?

What sorrow or pain do you wish to have comforted and healed?

Are you able to relinquish even your mistakes into God's hands to redeem?

Can you identify any loss or hurt that you are *not* yet willing to entrust to Jesus? What is holding you back from letting this go?

I call to You from the ends of the earth when my heart is without strength. Lead me to a rock that is high above me, for You have been a refuge for me. Psalm 61:2-3 HCSB

Show me a sign of Your goodness . . . because You, Lord, have helped and comforted me. Psalm 86:17 HCSB

What would you say to Jesus right now if you met Him face-to-face?

Words Spoken To The Heart

"Don't cry," He tenderly said. These words were not spoken to diminish her expression of grief or to minimize the emotional impact of her suffering, but were spoken out of compassion to convey comfort and hope. These reassuring words reflected a time in the future when "He will wipe away every tear from their eyes. There will be no more death or mourning or crying or pain, for the old order of things has passed away" (Revelation 21:4 NIV).

Though the coffin would have been considered unclean by Jewish Law, Jesus' compassion for this woman who had previously buried her husband and was about to bury her only son compelled Him to reach out and touch it. Jesus commanded the young man to get up!

The crowd was shocked to see the dead man sit up and talk! With tears in His eyes and a smile on His face, Jesus helped the bewildered man off the coffin platform and into his mother's open arms. Sounds of crying were replaced by expressions of shock and amazement and with shouts of praise and reverence. Soon boisterous chatter filled the air. Tears of grief turned to tears of joy as the reality began to sink in that they had just witnessed the restoration of this dead man! Imagine this mother's astonishment! Her only son was alive again!

Jesus' heart for widows and for those dealing with the loss of a child moved Him to raise a young man from the dead. Though the restored life was what the crowd was focused on, the impact on the individual woman was the most profound. This miracle demonstrated Jesus' kindhearted love for one grieving woman who faced an uncertain future without husband or son.

"Don't cry." Luke 7:13 NIV

Can you imagine how those words from Jesus affected the woman?

How do Jesus' words "don't cry" speak to *you*? Do they calm your fears?

"Blessed are those who mourn, for they will be comforted." Matthew 5:4 NIV

"And I will ask the Father, and He will give you another Counselor [Comforter, Helper, Intercessor, Advocate, Strengthener, and Standby] to be with you forever. He is the Spirit of truth." John 14:16-17 HCSB

Do you believe that Jesus is in the midst of your storms and giving you strength to endure them?

More importantly, do you believe that He can calm your storms?

Jesus got up and ordered the wind and the waves to be quiet. The wind stopped, and everything was calm. Jesus asked his disciples, "Why were you afraid? Don't you have any faith?" Mark 4:39-40 CEV

What does Jesus want you NOT to be afraid of — repercussions from broken relationships, death or your eternal security?

What specific things do you fear, but sense God wants you to relinquish into His loving care?

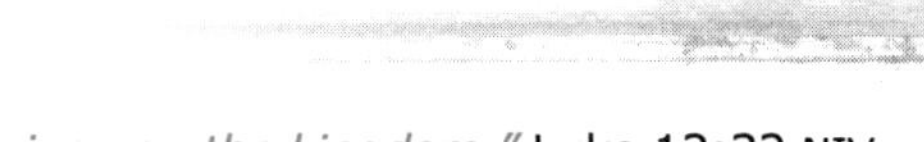

"Do not be afraid, little flock, for your Father has been pleased to give you the kingdom." Luke 12:32 NIV

"I tell you, my friends, do not be afraid of those who kill the body and after that can do no more." Luke 12:4 NIV

For those who have lost loved ones, the ultimate comfort comes with these words:

"I assure you: An hour is coming, and is now here, when the dead will hear the voice of the Son of God, and those who hear will live. For just as the Father has life in Himself, so also He has granted to the Son to have life in Himself." John 5:25-26 HCSB

What words of comfort would you like to hear from Jesus?

An Encounter With Jesus

Can you imagine the feelings this woman experienced? Her son was now fully alive! Was it all a dream? Who *was* this man who had so graciously restored *her* son to life? After the shock subsided, maybe the woman would focus on the events of the day. Who was this man who dared to touch a coffin, did not shun death and spoke life into a dead body? Why would He choose to revive her son? It was just too good to be true! Yet, it was only through the confirmation of her vibrant son and amazed friends that she realized that life had truly begun again.

The entire region was talking about this great prophet who appeared among them, but only she would appreciate the personal nature of the miracle that had been performed. It was witnessed by the masses, but was understood as an individual act of compassion for an anonymous woman.

Would she see Jesus again? Maybe. Maybe not. Regardless of whether she faced him again, she would confidently testify about the power and love of this man named Jesus, who looked with kindness upon a poor widow and comforted her with grace. Instead of facing a life of loneliness and uncertainty, she now felt safe and secure.

This blessed woman most likely lived with an inner joy birthed by a consuming awareness that Jesus redeemed her from a seemingly hopeless pit and crowned her with love through His compassionate miracle of the restoration of her son. Truly, God had come to her aid in a powerful and personal way.

How did this woman experience God during her loss and grief?

Have you experienced God during a season of sorrow? If not, can you identify why you felt alone during a dark time in your life?

Is there an area of your life's journey that you previously turned over to God and He resolved? Describe the outcome.

How did that experience bolster your faith in His personal hand on your life?

Guard me as the apple of Your eye; hide me in the shadow of Your wings. Psalm 17:8 HCSB

What fears would you like to entrust to Jesus' empathetic heart?

What fears do you *need* to entrust to Jesus, knowing that you are hesitating? Is it time to face these fears and ask for God's help to conquer them?

The Lord is my light and my salvation — whom shall I fear? The Lord is the stronghold of my life — of whom shall I be afraid? Psalm 27:1 NIV

They will have no fear of bad news; their hearts are steadfast, trusting in the Lord. Psalm 112:7 NIV

Their hearts are secure, they will have no fear. Psalm 112:8 NIV

How confident are you in Jesus' protective and comforting love for widows, fatherless, orphans and those who are helpless and defenseless?

Would you place yourself in any of those "categories"?

A father to the fatherless, a defender of widows, is God in his holy dwelling. Psalm 68:5 NIV

The Lord watches over the foreigner and sustains the fatherless and the widow, but he frustrates the ways of the wicked. Psalm 146:9 NIV

Even if my father and mother abandon me, the Lord cares for me. Psalm 27:10 HCSB

Are you looking to Jesus as your Provider? What physical needs are you relying on Him to provide — daily necessities, financial resources or safety?

Are you courageously asking Jesus to provide healing for your emotional scars and broken relationships?

What spiritual needs are you looking to Jesus to provide?

The Lord is with me; I will not be afraid. What can mere mortals do to me? Psalm 118:6 NIV

Even when I go through the darkest valley, I fear no danger, for you are with me; your rod and your staff — they comfort me. Psalm 23:4 HCSB

Whom do you choose to trust for your safety?

How has Jesus comforted and strengthened you in times of insecurity or fear?

I pray to you, Lord! You are my place of safety, and you are my choice in the land of the living. Psalm 142:5 CEV

Be my defender and protector! Keep your promise and save my life. Psalm 119:154 CEV

In peace I will lie down and sleep, for you alone, Lord, make me dwell in safety. Psalm 4:8 NIV

Are you able to use your story of God's faithfulness in your life to encourage others?

Do you believe God is prompting you to reach out to others in their time of need?

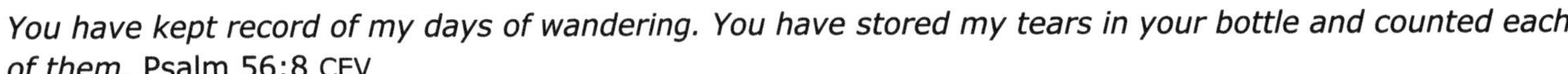

You have kept record of my days of wandering. You have stored my tears in your bottle and counted each of them. Psalm 56:8 CEV

You have turned my sorrow into joyful dancing. No longer am I sad and wearing sackcloth. I thank you from my heart, and I will never stop singing your praises, my LORD and my God. Psalm 30:11-12 CEV

Whom do you know that has recently suffered loss? How can you support that person through the grieving process?

In what ways can you help your grieving friend or family member experience Jesus' compassion?

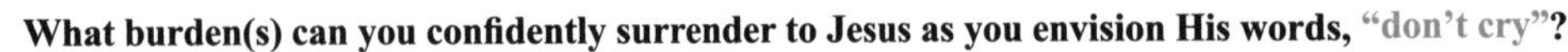

Cast your burden on the LORD, and He will support you; He will never allow the righteous to be shaken. Psalm 55:22 HCSB

Trust God, my friends, and always tell him each one of your concerns. God is our place of safety.Psalm 62:8 CEV

What burden(s) can you confidently surrender to Jesus as you envision His words, "don't cry"?

Your Encounter With Jesus

Jesus, what do You want me to know about your heart for *me*? Write what you are hearing Him say to you.

Is Jesus saying, **"Don't cry"**?

My Prayer For You

Compassionate Father, only You can see into the depths of this woman's heart and understand the source and intensity of her loss, pain, sorrow, grief and sadness. Come to her side and comfort her with Your words "don't cry," restoring her heart and life. Regardless of the circumstances that have made her feel helpless and insecure, may she continually feel the consoling safety of Your loving arms holding her close even in the darkest night and in the midst of a raging storm. Help her to understand that her heart's longing or loss will be restored in heaven. Show Yourself as her Provider, as she trusts in You. Give her Your heart for people so that others can be touched by Your compassion through her. In Your Son's name, Jesus, Amen!

Your Prayer

Thoughts Regarding Your Journey Experience

The Woman Who Loved Much

Luke 7:36-50

There comes a time in our lives when we recognize our mortality and begin to ask questions central to our existence. Why was I born? What is the purpose of my life? What happens when I die? Is there life after death? If so, how can I have eternal life? Is there a God? If God does exist, what does that mean to me? Who decides right and wrong? Am I being judged by how I live? Does it even matter?

Your Sins Are Forgiven.

The woman in this portrait undoubtedly asked some of those same questions and honestly admitted her human limitations and flawed standing in contrast to the perfectly divine Creator. Her repentant heart was convicted of her brokenness. She humbly sought forgiveness from the One she acknowledged had the power to forgive and provide reconciliation to the Eternal God. Forgiven of her sins, eternally secure and given a fresh start, this grateful woman expressed her love and devotion, publicly honoring Jesus.

In Her Shoes

A nameless woman heard that Jesus would be dining that evening at the home of Simon, a Pharisee. She must go to Him! Her desire to see Jesus was not borne out of a physical need such as a healing, and she did not have a request to make on behalf of a close family member. This yearning to be with Him was an intensely personal one that sprang from a heart convicted of her brokenness. Her deepest need was for forgiveness, which she believed He could bestow.

Though probably known by Simon, he certainly had not invited *her*, a woman AND a sinner. Regardless, she was determined to find Jesus. She knew that she would not be welcomed by Simon and his guests. In fact, she expected to be met with resistance because of her reputation in the town.

This woman was publicly branded as a sinner. Though the Biblical account does not specify how she received that status, most traditional interpretations of this story are quick to label this woman a prostitute. Though every person falls woefully short of perfection (thus, *all* have sinned), a prostituted woman would be an easy target of human condemnation because of her outwardly visible and identifiable failings. Because humans tend to classify sins and the degree of sinfulness, this woman was judged as an obvious sinner.

Those who were invited to the dinner gave disapproving stares as she approached. Simon's guests were not eager to cause a scene in front of Jesus, so they reluctantly allowed her to enter.

This marked woman was probably no stranger to abuse at the hands of men. So why would she seek out this man — Jesus? Maybe she had previously watched Him from afar and noticed that Jesus was profoundly different than any man she knew. He spoke with kindness and respect to every person, and surprisingly, He treated women with dignity. She was so tired of masking her shame, self-condemnation and loathing for the pit of existence she called life. Even though she felt unworthy and incapable of being "fixed," desperation fueled her search.

After finding Jesus at the table, she stood behind Him and quietly began to weep, her tears dripping down on His robe and feet. Her heart was overwhelmed with conviction of her human weakness and obvious flaws. She desperately wanted a new life. In an act of repentance and contrition she surrendered her regrets, mistakes and failed efforts at the feet of the One and only perfect being — the only One who had the love and power to forgive. Then she wept more, this time with gratitude.

This emotional outpouring was disconcerting for the host, but it was the intimacy of her proceeding actions that was shocking. Removing the covering of her head, this scorned woman wiped Jesus' moist feet with her hair, kissed them and then poured expensive perfume on them. To Simon, this was scandalous! How could Jesus allow a woman, specifically a *sinful* and *prostituted* woman, to touch Him in this way?

Jesus was well aware of the judging hearts of those witnessing this display of affection. With words for all to hear, He proceeded to tell Simon a parable about a moneylender who cancelled debts of two men. Simon correctly stated that the man whose debt was larger would love the moneylender more than the man with a smaller debt. Jesus had set the stage to deliver a profound lesson of forgiveness.

While Jesus conversed with the host, it seemed as though He was ignoring the woman, not even acknowledging her actions, shocking as they seemed. Then He turned toward her and prepared to speak again. The woman briefly looked up into His eyes, then dropped her head and continued with humility in repentant worship.

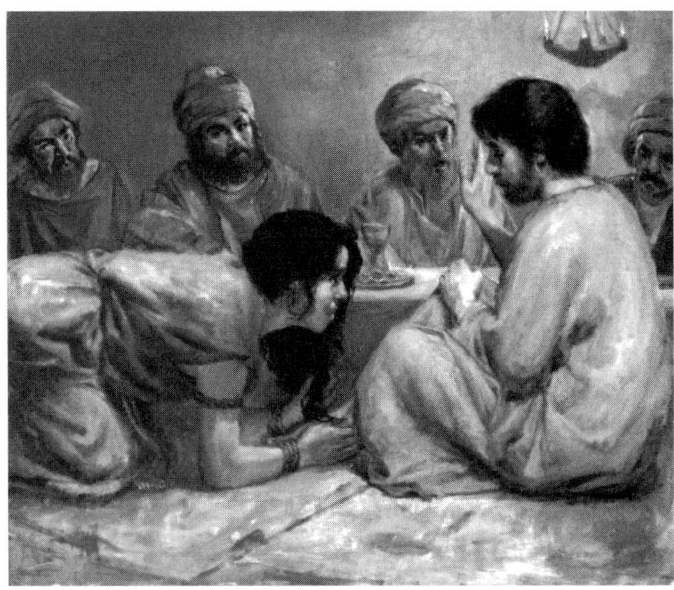

How do you relate to this woman? Do you relate to her reputation, pain and/or response to Jesus?

Why do you think she sought Jesus? How was He different than the other men she encountered during her life?

What is your understanding of "sin," as it relates to your life?

Have you acknowledged the reality of your temporary existence and certainty of death?

Describe your "smallness" in contrast to the power of nature and the immensity of the universe?

How vulnerable do you feel as a human? Explain your understanding of your position as a human in relation to an All-Powerful and Eternal God?

Are you comfortable or uncomfortable with this woman's display of emotion?

Face-To-Face With Jesus

In contrast to those in attendance at the dinner, Jesus had unique insight into this woman's heart and understanding of her motives. Looking through the sadness in her eyes, Jesus would have empathized with the despair brought about by selling one's body to be used for a man's pleasure. While others would assume that she willingly made a choice to become a prostitute, He alone would have perceived the circumstances which had drawn her into this demeaning lifestyle. Knowing that no woman ever dreams of or willingly seeks this powerless existence, His heart would ache for her rescue and restoration.

Jesus also understood the purity of her actions, which the other men judged to be indecent. Jesus saw a woman who had opened herself to public scrutiny with a display of emotional vulnerability. He could read her desperate and repentant heart and allowed this intimate expression of adoration.

It could be implied from the story that Jesus and she had previously met, and her sins were already forgiven. She understood that forgiveness by Jesus' grace and mercy was unearned and therefore, this expression of repentant worship was also an act of gratitude, a demonstration of the depth of her thankfulness to Jesus.

All sin, whether publicly visible or not, is a result of human nature straying or rebelling from God's will. This woman recognized her flawed nature and realized that there was nothing she could humanly do to measure up to the perfect and holy nature of God. Her conviction of sinfulness was intensified due to the public shame she endured. Jesus saw a woman emptied of herself, trusting Him to forgive and redeem. She was overwhelmed by His grace, compassion and mercy and worshipped at His feet.

Can you relate to this woman's publicly disgraced status and feelings of being devalued, overpowered, helpless or "stuck"?

Do you feel that your heart is similar to this woman's repentant heart?

Can you recall a specific time when you brought your brokenness to God and sought His forgiveness?

Has there been a time in your life when you "repented" — turned back toward God, instead of living a self-directed life not aligned to His intended will?

When Jesus looks through your eyes, does He see a humble heart? Or does He see a proud heart struggling to acknowledge your humanity in contrast to a perfect God?

Can you admit your human limitations and how short you fall when compared to the holiness of God?

We humans are only a breath; none of us are truly great. All of us together weigh less than a puff of air. Psalm 62:9 CEV

Honestly, do you have difficulty seeing the need for repentance because you consider yourself to be a "good person"?

Are you resistant to admitting your imperfections? Do you stubbornly attempt to defend your position with God?

Jesus is not threatened by your non-willingness or hesitation to surrender your will and turn to God for direction. He will always be there — patiently pursuing and waiting for you to choose to acknowledge your humanness and sinfulness.

None of us know our faults. Forgive me when I sin without knowing it. Psalm 19:12 CEV

Maybe you are at the opposite end of the spectrum, admitting "many sins." Deep within your heart do you believe that "He will never forgive me for what I've done"?

Maybe you are reading this book while incarcerated for a sin committed against a person or society. If this is your reality, what thoughts do you have regarding God's forgiveness?

If imprisoned, are you confident that you are forgiven in the eyes of God, even though living with punishment and consequences of a sinful action?

Would you categorize yourself as a "rebellious" person, jumping into sin, even when you know it is wrong and against God's will?

Be true to your name, Lord, by forgiving each one of my terrible sins. Psalm 25:11 CEV

Have you ever reached the point of being tired of pretending, tired of trying to be good, tired of doing life on your own?

Are you tired of trying to hide your brokenness or wounds? Drained from focusing on your shortcomings?

Are you weary from trying to hide the secrets in your heart? (Remember that God already knows and sees everything in your heart.)

Have you reached the end of yourself, with nothing to offer God except your desperation? "Lord, I am nothing and need You!"

Then I acknowledged my sin to You and did not conceal my iniquity. I said, "I will confess my transgressions to the Lord," and You took away the guilt of my sin. Psalm 32:5 HCSB

What do you need to be forgiven of? What are you most ashamed of? An affair, abortion or addiction?

Why is it so difficult to let go of this brokenness? Trust that Jesus is big enough to handle your brokenness and unloveliness. He sees and knows — and still loves.

Are you willing to stop the direction you are going and turn or return to God? Explain what has made you reach this point.

Would you like to receive Jesus' forgiveness and ask for a fresh start in life?

Be gracious to me, God, according to Your faithful love; according to Your abundant compassion, blot out my rebellion. Wash away my guilt, and cleanse me from my sin. For I am conscious of my rebellion, and my sin is always before me. Psalm 51:1-3 HCSB

Was there a specific point in time when the scriptures above were ones you wholeheartedly prayed?

Recall your journey of repentance and acceptance of the loving forgiveness of Jesus.

Turn to me and be gracious to me, for I am lonely and afflicted. Relieve the troubles of my heart and free me from my anguish. Look upon my affliction and my distress and take away all my sins. Psalm 25:16-18 NIV

Has someone told you that you are worthless and you now feel unworthy, dirty, broken and sick beyond repair? Have you believed this as truth, or lies?

Maybe you are having difficulty trusting in Jesus because He was a man — and you have suffered at the hands of a man. Are you learning about Jesus' divine love for you through His example of kindness and genuine tenderness to the women He met while walking the earth?

Regardless of your situation: Are you ready to offer all of yourself "to be fixed," to be healed of your brokenness, to be made whole and live in freedom?

Remember, Lord, Your compassion and Your faithful love, for they [have existed] from antiquity. Do not remember the sins of my youth or my acts of rebellion; in keeping with Your faithful love, remember me because of Your goodness, Lord. Psalm 25:6-7 HCSB

What would you like to say face-to-face to Jesus?

Words Spoken To The Heart

Jesus challenged Simon to acknowledge "this woman" and recounted the acts of devotion she had shown. He pointed out that Simon, as host, did not even perform the basic courtesies for a guest, yet "this woman" went above and beyond in a display of affection. Though Simon may have judged her actions as immoral because of her tainted reputation, Jesus did not interpret "this woman's" display as sensual in nature, but as an intimate expression of spiritual worship. He elevated the status of "this woman" by drawing attention to her example of devotion.

Jesus did not make her feel embarrassed for expressing heartfelt gratitude or minimize her emotional outburst. Her tears did not intimidate him and He was comfortable with a woman, even this prostituted one, touching Him, though others considered her actions inappropriate. Jesus did not react to her reputation, or to her past, but saw her in the present, in her entirety — not solely as a woman, but as a worshipper with a heart's expression of thankfulness bubbling over into this intimate act of reverence.

Jesus made another shocking statement to Simon by announcing that her sins (which admittedly, were many) had been forgiven because "she loved much." Her demonstration of adoration was in response to forgiveness He could bestow and to the respect with which she was treated. With courage and boldness, this woman took the initiative to move toward Jesus, publicly worshipping and expressing her love toward Him while risking even greater adverse societal reaction.

Next, He addressed the woman by confirming that her "sins had been forgiven," not because of her actions, but because of who He is. Her faith in Him had saved her. Just as He told the woman with chronic bleeding, "go in peace," He welcomed this humble and grateful woman, this sinful and disgraced woman, into His fellowship by these words, and then sent her away with a blessing. By His kind response, He elevated the status of this social outcast, using her as an example of repentant and grateful worship.

"Your sins are forgiven." "Your faith has saved you; go in peace." Luke 7:48, 50 NIV

How did Jesus' words *"your sins are forgiven"* affect and change this woman?

How do these words from Jesus speak to *your* heart?

"Suppose one of you has a hundred sheep and loses one of them. Doesn't he leave the ninety-nine in the open country and go after the lost sheep until he finds it? And when he finds it, he joyfully puts it on his shoulders and goes home. Then he calls his friends and neighbors together and says, 'Rejoice with me; I have found my lost sheep.' I tell you that in the same way there will be more rejoicing in heaven over one sinner who repents than over ninety-nine righteous persons who do not need to repent." Luke 15:4-7 NIV

Every human being has been "lost," wandering in the opposite direction from God. Only through the loving grace and forgiveness of Jesus is it possible to turn back to God and restore the relationship with our Creator.

"Or suppose a woman has ten silver coins and loses one. Doesn't she light a lamp, sweep the house and search carefully until she finds it? And when she finds it, she calls her friends and neighbors together and says, 'Rejoice with me; I have found my lost coin.' In the same way, I tell you, there is rejoicing in the presence of the angels of God over one sinner who repents." Luke 15:8-10 NIV

Through Jesus comes reconciliation with our heavenly Father.
He desires it — do you?

Do you believe it is possible — even for you?

Are you convinced that you are forgiven? Do you feel forgiven?

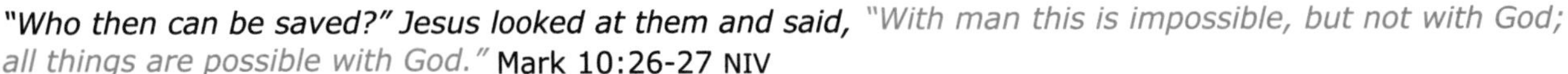

"Who then can be saved?" Jesus looked at them and said, "With man this is impossible, but not with God; all things are possible with God." Mark 10:26-27 NIV

"The time has come," he said. "The kingdom of God is near. Repent and believe the good news!" Mark 1:15 NIV

What do Jesus' words *"your faith has saved you"* mean to you? Faith — in what? Or is it faith — in Whom?

Are you saved by your "goodness" or by belief and trust in Jesus — that He is the only One with the authority and power to forgive and save?

"All people of every nation must be told in my name to turn to God, in order to be forgiven." Luke 24:47 CEV

Jesus also said, *"Go in peace."* Why would peace follow forgiveness?

Have you experienced God's gift of peace in your life after receiving the past, present and future forgiveness of your sins?

Why would receiving peace be important to Jesus?

"I give you peace, the kind of peace that only I can give. It isn't like the peace that this world can give. So don't be worried or afraid." John 14:27 CEV

Do you believe that Jesus was "merely" a man? Or do you believe that Jesus is the Son of God?

What difference does that distinction make to your life?

Which is easier: to say to the paralytic, 'Your sins are forgiven,' or to say, 'Get up, pick up your stretcher, and walk'? But so you may know that the Son of Man has authority on earth to forgive sins," He told the paralytic, *"I tell you: get up, pick up your stretcher, and go home."* Mark 2:9-11 HCSB

Jesus desires to restore spiritual and human relationships and instructs us that forgiveness is the key. He set the example for forgiveness and expects us to do the same for others.

Peter came up to the Lord and asked, "How many times should I forgive someone who does something wrong to me? Is seven times enough?" Jesus answered: "Not just seven times, but seventy-seven times!" Matthew 18:21-22 CEV

"That is how my Father in heaven will treat you, if you don't forgive each of my followers with all your heart." Matthew 18:35 CEV

Jesus set the ultimate example of forgiving others (when nailed to a cross as a falsely-accused criminal) and spoke the following words:

Jesus said, "Father, forgive these people! They don't know what they're doing." Luke 23:34 CEV

Why is forgiving others so difficult?

But why is forgiveness important to both human and spiritual relationships?

What message of forgiveness would you like to hear from Jesus?

An Encounter With Jesus

What did this woman's life look like after her encounter with Jesus? She was free! Forgiven! Life would never be the same for her, as she experienced a new beginning. She was a transformed person, no longer burdened with guilt and condemnation, but confident of her standing in the eyes of God.

Jesus' forgiveness (for past, present and future sins) would radically change her life and most likely she would become one of His followers in response to the mercy she was shown. This woman could testify that Jesus loved her unconditionally and there are no faults or mistakes (no matter how bad or horrible) that are too far from His gracious touch.

Although her reputation may always have been tainted, no longer did she feel the weight of shame from her past. Jesus' public comments had restored her status in His eyes and that was all that mattered. She would embark along a new path and over time this purity of heart that reflected repentance and gratitude would translate to a purified life, now lovingly walking in the direction of God's will.

How was this woman treated differently by Jesus? Did His interaction affect her response?

How did this woman experience God? Describe her response to the forgiveness she received.

How would you describe "grace" in light of what this woman experienced?

Our God, you bless everyone whose sins you forgive and wipe away. You bless them by saying, "You told me your sins, without trying to hide them, and now I forgive you." Psalm 32:1-2 CEV

For as high as the heavens are above the earth, so great is His faithful love toward those who fear Him. As far as the east is from the west, so far has He removed our transgressions from us. As a father has compassion on his children, so the LORD has compassion on those who fear Him. For He knows what we are made of, remembering that we are dust. Psalm 103:11-14 HCSB

Do you believe that *all* your sins have been forgiven, your guilt removed and that you stand before your Creator cleansed and free?

How have you experienced God's forgiveness? Do you believe that Jesus has forgiven you by His grace?

What is your response to forgiveness offered to you by Jesus?

Do you "love much"? How do you express your gratitude to Him?

Lord, if You considered sins, Lord, who could stand? But with You there is forgiveness, so that You may be revered. Psalm 130:3-4 HCSB

Once forgiven, what is your attitude toward forgiving others?

Is there anyone you need to forgive? Ask Jesus to release any bitterness towards them, then genuinely and graciously forgive.

Maybe you still need to forgive yourself — Jesus has! Or in some way, do you need to forgive God?

Are you "at peace" with your standing in God's eyes?

Can you say with confident assurance that you have been forgiven by Jesus and your relationship with God is forever reconciled?

The Lord is good and upright; therefore He shows sinners the way. Psalm 25:8 HCSB

He renews my life; He leads me along the right paths for His name's sake. Psalm 23:3 HCSB

What is the outcome of hearing Jesus say, "Go in peace" to you?

YOUR ENCOUNTER WITH JESUS

Jesus, what do You want me to understand by this repentant woman's example? Write what you are hearing Him say to you.

Is He saying, **"Your sins are forgiven"**?

Can you hear Jesus saying, **"Your faith has saved you; go in peace"**?

MY PRAYER FOR YOU

Lord, only You have the ability to look into our hearts and lives and see how profoundly incomplete and flawed we are. Only You can open our eyes to see our lack of perfection and sinfulness in contrast to Your perfect and holy nature. Please gently and lovingly allow this woman to see herself through Your eyes — human, incomplete, flawed and sinful, yet divinely loved and eternally forgiven. Give her the courage to surrender to Your will for her life. Please help her to experience the freedom of Your forgiveness and Your gift of peace. Also fill her with your gracious nature so that she will forgive others, as You have forgiven her. Only in Jesus' name can we pray this. Amen!

YOUR PRAYER

Thoughts Regarding Your Journey Experience

A Lesson About Priorities

Luke 10:38-42

Who doesn't relate to this story of a busy and competent, yet overwhelmed and worried woman named Martha? Our daily "to-do list" seems to suck the peace and joy out of us, as we struggle to keep our lives organized and somewhat in control. So many of us wake up early, hit the ground running and collapse at the end of the day. We long for a brief reprieve from our numerous responsibilities and torrid pace.

One Thing Is Essential.

Do we recognize the worries and distractions of the heart that distance us from Jesus? There must be more to life. Martha longed for relief and was reminded about what was most important in life. This multi-layered lesson about identity, worry and rest proves to be liberating for us all.

In Her Shoes

Oh, there was so much preparation to take place prior to the dinner that evening! And this would be no ordinary dinner, as many additional guests were expected because word of Jesus' visit had spread throughout the town. Martha was concerned that she would not be ready for the festivities to begin in a few hours. The arrival of Jesus always brought excitement, but the responsibility for the meal and welcoming the guests fell on Martha's shoulders because she had opened up her home for the gathering. Jesus was a special and honored guest, and she wanted to make sure all the details of His visit were arranged and that the company enjoyed themselves. Martha took her role of hostess seriously and was well-known for being diligent, conscientious and efficient, rarely sitting or resting from all of her household duties.

After greeting Jesus and His disciples at the door, Martha led them to the courtyard to relax prior to the meal. Her sister Mary was also excited that Jesus had arrived and sat down where she could hear every word that He spoke.

Martha looked outside the kitchen area where Jesus and the disciples had congregated. She could see that her sister Mary was sitting at His feet listening intently to His words. Just when Martha had needed her sister's assistance, Mary joined Jesus in conversation. "Doesn't she understand how much I need her to help me?" Martha muttered to herself. Part of her wanted to be with the others as they conversed with Jesus, but she felt responsible for the upcoming meal and there simply was no time to spare.

Martha tried to get Mary's attention and motion for her to come to the kitchen. However, Mary was focused on Jesus and unaware of Martha's growing irritation. With each glance at Mary, Martha's frustration increased. She assumed that it would not seem inappropriate for her to ask Jesus to direct Mary to help her. After all, women were the ones responsible for making and serving the meal, and she needed support if this evening were to be a success. Jesus would certainly understand her request.

Finally, unable to remain silent any longer, Martha approached Jesus and indignantly blurted out, "Lord, don't You care that my sister has left me to do the work by myself? Tell her to come and help me!"

In what ways do you relate to Martha?

Do you have a reputation as a "doer," with the gift of hospitality and ability to multi-task?

Are you known to be competent, with many accomplishments credited to you?

Do you consider yourself a perfectionist or have the tendency to over commit?

Like Martha, is your life also fraught with busyness and distractions? Describe the areas of your life that consume your time.

What do you think was the source of Martha's frustration with her sister Mary?

Would you prefer to identify with Mary, but honestly do not think it is realistic to find time to "sit with Jesus," considering that "a woman's work is never done"?

Face-To-Face With Jesus

Jesus glanced up to meet the glare of Martha and heard her request. He had been watching her bustle within the house making preparations and was not surprised by her outburst. Martha was His friend and had served Him on several occasions because she had a servant's heart and gift for hospitality.

But Martha's tendency toward worrying about the details of the household, though admirable, had created a driven, efficient and somewhat controlling woman whose identity was wrapped up in her reputation as an expert hostess. Martha was never finished with her chores and seemed to be a perfectionist who was continually able to find additional tasks to perform in her household. One look through her eyes, Jesus could see how perturbed and annoyed she was with her sister who had chosen to spend time with Him rather than with the serving duties. Martha was no longer serving with a compassionate heart, but with an agitated one. She was weary and burdened, but seemingly could not afford to take time to rest.

Only Jesus could truly identify the deeper issues that were the source of Martha's irritation. Maybe Martha was judging her sister to be less diligent according to society's expectations of women's roles within the household. Or she could have been feeling overwhelmed by the seemingly endless tasks she was responsible for. Martha was not able to acknowledge Mary's student heart, and it seemed the focus of her concern was more out of frustration that she was bearing the load of the work, rather than disappointment that she was unable to sit at Jesus' feet, too. Though she wouldn't admit it, Martha may have been jealous of her sister.

Looking into Martha's heart, Jesus could see a woman trying to find fulfillment in serving others, but empty from neglecting the true source of fulfillment — time with Him. He knew her fulfillment in this physical life would never be complete, but would come through "resting in *Him*," sitting at His feet and gaining the spiritual nourishment that her burdened heart needed.

It was time for a lesson about priorities.

How would you summarize Jesus' main concerns when He looked into Martha's heart?

In light of Martha's story, what does Jesus see when He looks into *your* heart?

Do any of these honest thoughts occasionally surface in your heart?

My life is out of control.
I have no one to help me.
People will think less of me if I don't get this done.
I have to work hard to control my life.
I don't need to rest. That's what lazy people do.
I'm judged by what I get done.
No one else can do the job correctly.
I have no extra time.
I feel guilty when I don't pray or read the Bible.
My best is never good enough.
I don't need God's help.
Don't people understand how busy I am?
I'm so stressed out.
How am I ever going to make it?
Life is overwhelming right now.
I'm surrounded by incompetents.
I'm so tired.
I feel so disconnected from God.
I'm busy, but I'm supposed to be using my gifts.
I don't even know how to pray right now.
I have to be perfect and make my world perfect.
I must achieve bigger and better things.
I have to be in control to get what I want.

Can you identify the underlying reasons behind your agreement with any of these statements?

How long will I store up anxious concerns within me, agony in my mind every day? Psalm 13:2 HCSB

How is life overwhelming at times? Are you continually hurried or rushed?

Would you admit to being a "complainer"? Are you frequently in a negative mood? If so, can you identify why?

Are you tired of pretending you have it all pulled together, wearing a smile as a mask while hiding what is held in your heart?

Do you see the need to simplify your life, or do you keep telling yourself it is impossible because of your circumstances?

Do you wish for the ability or courage to say "no" more often?

When my spirit grows faint within me, it is you who know my way. Psalm 142:3 NIV

Could your competence and independence be standing in your way of admitting your need for an adjustment in life's priorities?

Does it seem like "non-productive" time to pursue spiritual matters?

Does Jesus have second-place status in your life — getting your leftover time after the chores and responsibilities are completed?

Describe your excuses for not spending time with Jesus.

Are service opportunities creating distance from Jesus?

Are you a procrastinator and find it difficult to spend time with God?

Are you resisting Jesus in any way? Do you have the tendency to think you know it all or have it all figured out?

Search me, O God, and know my heart; test me and know my anxious thoughts. Psalm 139:23 NIV

Truly, how much do you want to think like God, take on His nature and walk with Him? Describe your commitment to Jesus.

Do you view Jesus as your Master and continually want to learn from Him?

What worries and anxieties would you like to surrender to Jesus?

Are you able to surrender ALL your cares, including your fears, to Him?

Would you like to raise the "white flag" of surrender and ask Jesus for help to reprioritize your life?

Words Spoken To The Heart

"Martha, Martha," He said in a friendly and loving tone, gracefully trying to settle her down while overlooking her judgmental and demanding attitude. She was "worried and upset" about many things. As the guest and recipient of her hospitality, His tone seemed to communicate His understanding of her tendency to become consumed with her "to-do list," yet He wanted to relieve her from the expectations to be the "perfect hostess" and help her understand how life should be prioritized.

Jesus would also be concerned with the distractions and irritations that caused Martha to make demands of Him and lash out at her sister. Martha's gift of serving was tainted if done with a judgmental attitude or with words of bitterness or self-pity.

"There is only one thing that is necessary and Mary has chosen the right thing," Jesus added, validating the choice her sister had made. His statement that Mary had made the better choice raised the status of women by validating their desire to pursue spiritual matters as students of Jesus, rather than exclusively playing the expected servant role. Jesus would break with societal tradition by encouraging women to focus on spiritual matters by allowing them to share in conversations typically reserved for men. Though life's responsibilities would still remain, the value of women increased as Jesus made a statement regarding the equality of access to Jesus and spiritual teaching.

Even though Jesus was the recipient of Martha's serving heart, He was telling her that it was more important to spend time with the eternal things than get overly wrought about physical things, such as meal preparation. Jesus did not seem to discourage service, in itself, but cautioned Martha not to allow the busyness, even if done in service to Him, to affect her priorities. Worldly pursuits are temporal, whereas spiritual pursuits have eternal consequences.

Jesus would have preferred for Martha to be sitting at His feet, as well, rather than being consumed by the busyness of serving Him. He would have preferred her presence, her heart for *Him*, and her time with Him. In essence, Jesus gave her permission to simplify and prioritize her life so that she too, would seek the one thing that is necessary, or essential — sitting at the Lord's feet, listening to Him, enjoying His company, sharing life's adventures — experiencing Him!

Jesus may have also implied that Martha had become obsessed with additional details of serving — even frivolous ones. Maybe she was busy with trivial tasks and chores that, if analyzed, could be jettisoned for the more important time of being in worship at Jesus' feet and listening to His words.

By Jesus' response, He reminded Martha not to neglect the *relationship* — the desire for growing closer to Him — as there is no substitute, not even with the good works of serving. Perhaps Martha wrapped her identity in being a *doer*, but her identity and true fulfillment would come from time *with* Jesus.

"Martha, Martha, you are worried and upset about many things, but only one thing is needed. Mary has chosen what is better, and it will not be taken away from her." Luke 10:41-42 NIV

Why do you think Jesus said Martha's name twice?

What tone of voice do you imagine Jesus used with Martha?

Do you hear Jesus' concern for His friend Martha in His words?

How did those words spoken by Jesus affect or change Martha?

How do these words regarding worry and anxiety resonate with you?

Jesus said to his disciples, "Don't be worried! Have faith in God and have faith in me." John 14:1 CEV

Then He said to His disciples: "Therefore I tell you, don't worry about your life, what you will eat; or about the body, what you will wear. For life is more than food and the body more than clothing. Consider the ravens: they don't sow or reap; they don't have a storeroom or a barn; yet God feeds them. Aren't you worth much more than the birds? Can any of you add a cubit to his height by worrying? If then you're not able to do even a little thing, why worry about the rest? Consider how the wildflowers grow: they don't labor or spin thread. Yet I tell you, not even Solomon in all his splendor was adorned like one of these! If that's how God clothes the grass, which is in the field today and is thrown into the furnace tomorrow, how much more will He do for you—you of little faith?" Luke 12:22-28 HCSB

What are the "many things" you are worried and anxious about?

What specifically are you "obsessing" over? What do you find yourself complaining about?

Are you worried about bills, instability with your job, loss of your house, no place to call home, concerned about your marriage, your kids or your safety?

Are you frazzled, with too much to do and too little time, while playing multiple roles — wife, mother, employee and caregiver?

So don't worry, saying, 'What will we eat?' or 'What will we drink?' or 'What will we wear?' For the idolaters eagerly seek all these things, and your heavenly Father knows that you need them. But seek first the kingdom of God and His righteousness, and all these things will be provided for you. Therefore don't worry about tomorrow, because tomorrow will worry about itself. Each day has enough trouble of its own." Matthew 6:31-34 HCSB

Are you emotionally burdened because you struggle to trust that God will take care of your needs?

Are you unable to "let go" of your control and give your circumstances to God?

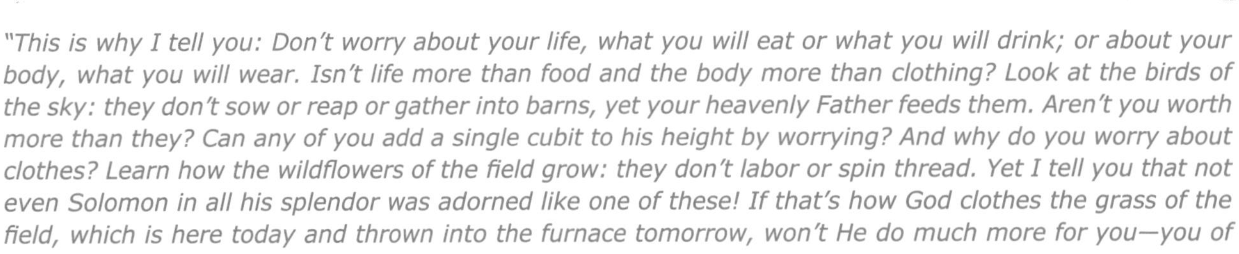

"This is why I tell you: Don't worry about your life, what you will eat or what you will drink; or about your body, what you will wear. Isn't life more than food and the body more than clothing? Look at the birds of the sky: they don't sow or reap or gather into barns, yet your heavenly Father feeds them. Aren't you worth more than they? Can any of you add a single cubit to his height by worrying? And why do you worry about clothes? Learn how the wildflowers of the field grow: they don't labor or spin thread. Yet I tell you that not even Solomon in all his splendor was adorned like one of these! If that's how God clothes the grass of the field, which is here today and thrown into the furnace tomorrow, won't He do much more for you—you of little faith?" Matthew 6:25-30 HCSB

Do you define your identity by your achievements, resume, ability to make money, career and reputation (perhaps as an organizer or manager)?

Do you pride yourself in your talents, ability to organize and accomplish projects, or with being a "doer"?

Is your "busyness" an attempt to grasp significance or a cover for internal turmoil that you are trying to suppress?

Are you basing your identity on who society says you are, or on who Jesus says you are?

Are you trying to gain Jesus' attention and favor by your good deeds?

Do you think that Jesus will be happier with you because of your service?

Do you need to be reminded that Jesus loves you unconditionally — that there is nothing you can do to earn God's love?

"All of you, take up My yoke and learn from Me, because I am gentle and humble in heart, and you will find rest for yourselves. For My yoke is easy and My burden is light." Matthew 11:29-30 HCSB

When you feel insignificant and overlooked — even within your busyness — does it make you irritable toward others?

Have you lost your ability to be compassionate because you are so determined to get your "to-do list" done?

Could Martha's irritation come from her jealousy of Mary — that Mary had Jesus' attention instead of her?

Can you see how unsettling this may have been for Martha — to realize that her identity of "doing" was not achieving the results she expected?

"Don't keep striving for what you should eat and what you should drink, and don't be anxious. For the Gentile world eagerly seeks all these things, and your Father knows that you need them. But seek His kingdom, and these things will be provided for you. Don't be afraid, little flock, because your Father delights to give you the kingdom." Luke 12:29-32 HCSB

How does your "worry" affect others? Have your concerns and anxieties affected your ability to love and be patient with the people around you?

Martha's tone of voice could be construed as self-righteous or judgmental because she had allowed worries to put her in a negative frame of mind. Is that one of Jesus' lessons He would like for you to learn from this story?

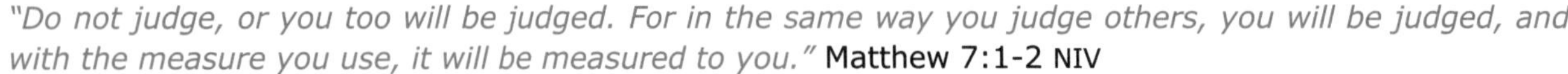

"Do not judge, or you too will be judged. For in the same way you judge others, you will be judged, and with the measure you use, it will be measured to you." Matthew 7:1-2 NIV

We are expected to use our talents, time and money wisely, but can you honestly admit your life is prioritized first around your relationship with Jesus?

Under what circumstances does your heart become distanced from Jesus? What small gods are you distracted by?

Do you recognize that you might need to "rest" from your doing, striving, obtaining, controlling and leading?

Can you see that you may need to relinquish your independence, self-reliance, maybe even self-importance, and reprioritize your focus and use of your time?

Has your busyness, even in service to the church and people, crowded out time with Jesus?

"Come with me by yourselves to a quiet place and get some rest." Mark 6:31 NIV

Is Jesus saying to you:

"These people honor Me with their lips, but their heart is far from Me." Matthew 15:8 HCSB

"Not everyone who says to me, 'Lord, Lord,' will enter the kingdom of heaven, but only the one who does the will of my Father who is in heaven. Many will say to me on that day, 'Lord, Lord, did we not prophesy in your name and in your name drive out demons and in your name perform many miracles?' Then I will tell them plainly, 'I never knew you.'" Matthew 7:21-23 NIV

"I never knew YOU." (And more importantly), You, dear woman, don't know ME — you missed the point of life — ME! Jesus desires a *relationship* with you. He delights in your longing to spend time with Him, learning about Him and becoming more like Him.

A woman can be busy doing numerous good deeds, good service, and even in God's name. This lesson reminds us that while on earth we should choose the better values, the eternal ones. Is it time to reassess your motivation for all of your activities, including serving?

Have you addressed the motivation for your busyness? Who are you trying to please?

Are you striving to be well-esteemed by society because social activism is currently fashionable? Are you striving for human recognition, maybe even within your church?

Are you involved with serving projects to earn God's favor?

Or can you truly say that you serve because God has given you a heart for serving people?

How has your understanding about serving Jesus changed through Martha's story?

Maybe it is not your *use of time* that has caused distance between Jesus and you, but your *frame of mind* that is clouded with worries and anxieties. Jesus desires for us to be settled, at peace with Him and others.

Do you need time with Jesus — to be refilled and refocused — so that you can go out again and serve His people with His compassionate perspective?

"Come to Me, all you who are weary and burdened, and I will give you rest." Matthew 11:28 HCSB

What do you sense Jesus is saying to you regarding your priorities?

An Encounter With Jesus

Later in Scripture, we find Martha serving Jesus again, so it was not the *serving* itself that Jesus was addressing. Jesus exposed the heart of the issue — the busyness and emotional comparisons that caused Martha to be worried and upset, as well as crowding out time to be with Him. Jesus had given Martha permission to *prioritize her relationship* with Him. Her household work would always be there — and would get done. But first, she was reminded to arrange to find time to sit at Jesus' feet and learn from Him, as Mary did. He encouraged her to "rest in Him," as she was weary from carrying many burdens.

Martha learned that her identity should be based in Jesus, not in her achievements, efficiency or reputation. Jesus gave her value and worth from being with Him. This value was not based on secular standards of the world, but from eternal values that will not fade away.

Maybe after the conversation, with her priorities straight and realization of her need to have her identity in Jesus, Martha timed her serving and used it as a gift for compassionately serving others, not as a means of defining who she was. Jesus had taught her that even servants can lose focus on the bigger picture, so she would find time to rise above the busyness of the everyday to focus on eternity.

Hopefully, Martha relinquished some of her perfectionist tendencies in order to allow time to sit at Jesus' feet with His other disciples. She continued to serve, but perhaps she moderated her tendency to be consumed and overwhelmed with her daily "to-do list" and concentrated on her heart-to-heart intimacy with Jesus. She learned that Jesus desired to walk with her — as she focused *on Him* rather than rushing off to do something *for Him*. He was more interested in their *relationship* than on her *performance*.

And in the process of walking with Jesus, perhaps the underlying emotional reasons for causing Martha to be "worried and upset" were addressed. Underlying irritants were exposed and an apology to her sister restored their relationship.

The lesson of priorities pierced Martha's heart when she heard of Jesus' death. Every moment spent with Him was precious; every word He had spoken burned in her heart. Though the meals she provided had faded away, the relationship with her Lord would remain forever. She had learned that Jesus was central to her life, out of which all of her activities, including service to others, flowed.

How did Martha experience Jesus that day?

Have you experienced Jesus in a similar way?

This lesson about priorities is not given to shame or condemn us for not making time to spend with Jesus. The message is that Jesus loves you and desires to share Himself with you. He desires to spend time with you in an eternal relationship.

We are reminded that our **identity** should be in Jesus. After our "being" is focused on Him, our "doing" will become an expression of His love. Serving will not come primarily from a sense of duty or obligation, but from a heart transformed, filled full and overflowing with the love of Jesus for His people. Acts of service will come from the heart, reflecting a life that responds to the needs of family, friends, neighbors and community as Jesus would and because He commanded us to love others.

If our identity is in Jesus, we will look to Him as our Teacher and Master and desire to learn from Him by remaining in His presence. Humans may have nuggets of truth, but only Jesus IS Truth.

Teach me Your way, Lord, and I will live by Your truth. Psalm 86:11 HCSB

Surely you desire truth in the inner parts; you teach me wisdom in the inmost place. Psalm 51:6 NIV

This lesson is also about **rest**, not only in the typical sense of physical rest, but also the quality of being settled before Jesus, freed from anxiety and the cares of this world. Rest implies a contented heart that puts trust in God alone. A heart at rest relinquishes control, futile attempts to be perfect and resentment that comes from judging others.

In that context what would it mean for you to rest?

Describe the concept of "rest" and how would that look for you?

Do you need more sleep or time to take a walk?

Do you wish for an uncluttered, private area to pray, read God's words and worship? Probably more accurately, do you long for time to rest in God's presence?

Are you a mother - on call 24 hours a day, 7 days a week? This intense season of your life can be the most demanding on a woman's time, especially if you also have employment responsibilities.

Do you need to ask Jesus to help facilitate your commitment to Him?

I am at rest in God alone; my salvation comes from Him. He alone is my rock and my salvation, my stronghold; I will never be shaken. Psalm 62:1-2 HCSB

Many women are actively involved in areas of service to the church and community, in addition to family duties. What obligations, including service activities, do you need to jettison?

Jesus desires for you to be settled, not worried or anxious. What areas in your life would you like to feel more peace?

Where do you need permission from Jesus to let go? Do you need to be encouraged to say "no" more often?

Turn my eyes from looking at what is worthless; give me life in Your ways. Psalm 119:37 HCSB

Does Martha's lesson encourage you to find ways to simplify your life? Do you need to simplify your family's life as well?

What specific areas in your life are you determined to reprioritize?

Do you have any specific thoughts on how you can adjust your schedule to spend time with Jesus?

Could this be a "Martha prayer"?

Jesus, forgive me for neglecting our relationship. Please give me permission to rest in You. Let me know it's ok to say "no" to areas that weigh me down and take away my time with You. Renew my heart. Help me to know when and where to spend my time and to know the difference between serving for the sake of serving and serving You. I recognize the gifts and talents You have given me and desire to use them to Your glory, but please help me not to be confused as to what is eternally important. Settle my heart and give me faith to give all my concerns and worries to You. Help me to be content to sit at your feet and draw my identity from You. Please give me a stronger desire to learn from You, my Teacher and Master.

"Anyone who loves their life will lose it, while anyone who hates their life in this world will keep it for eternal life. Whoever serves me must follow me; and where I am, my servant also will be. My Father will honor the one who serves me." John 12:25-26 NIV

"For even the Son of Man did not come to be served, but to serve, and to give His life — a ransom for many." Mark 10:45 HCSB

What would you like to say to Jesus regarding this multi-layered lesson about priorities?

Your Encounter With Jesus

Jesus, what are You trying to teach me through Your friend Martha's story? Write what you are hearing Him say to you.

Is Jesus saying, **"Only one thing is essential"**?

My Prayer For You

Lord, gently remind this dear woman not to be controlled by the physical demands of her life, but to live with Your eternal perspective in the forefront of her mind. You loved her first. Help her to wholeheartedly love You first by organizing her priorities to sit intentionally in Your presence. Help her to trust You completely with her worries and anxieties and give her an eternal perspective of life. Remind her that she is nothing without You and that her identity should be in You. And when she serves, refocus her heart to purposefully bring glory to You and Your name. Let her be a beacon for those who are worried and anxious, as she encourages others to rest in You. This I pray in Jesus' name! Amen!

Your Prayer

Thoughts Regarding Your Journey Experience

The Deliverance Of A Crippled Woman

Luke 13:10-17

Like many individuals, the woman in this portrait lived for many years with a debilitating health issue. She accepted her physical reality and determined to live life as normally as possible, relying on her faith to sustain flagging hope. What would it have been like to be seen and pursued by Jesus, then blessed as the recipient of His restoring power? With a disabled woman on center stage, Jesus taught a lesson about the value and beauty of human life, emphasizing the created intent that humans live fully and freely. He demonstrated that His mission was to deliver people from all forms of oppression and injustice.

You Are Set Free.

In Her Shoes

Jesus was in town! A woman heard He was teaching in the synagogue, so she got up early on Sabbath morning to allow extra time for the journey. Though controversy seemed to follow Him, she wondered if Jesus could possibly be the prophesied Messiah. You see, for a woman who had been crippled by an evil spirit, the Messiah was her only hope. Though she had lived with physical limitations for eighteen years, it was hearing the Scriptures read in the synagogue that took her mind off her ever-present pain and hopeless circumstances.

The evil spirit tormented her emotionally, as well, and most likely she battled depression and discouragement. Though it was difficult to make the trek from her home, she attended the synagogue regularly for comfort, inspiration and peace. She found respite for her troubled soul by listening to the Scriptures. Maybe one of her favorites was Isaiah 58:8 that spoke of a time when healing would quickly appear or Zephaniah 3:19 that promised God's rescue of the lame.

Like so many individuals with a disability or deformity, she lived day-to-day quietly resigned to her situation, with no expectation of relief. With each passing year her body deteriorated, the pain increased and mobility decreased. Her muscles seemed frozen in a position that was bent at the waist and she was unable to straighten up. Walking was tedious. She used canes for stability and to periodically lean on for rest. Even daily activities, like preparing a meal, took extra time and were exhausting. Sadly, many years had passed since she was able to participate completely in her family's activities. Oh, how she longed to pick up a child again!

Today she had tried to leave her home earlier than usual so she could find a place toward the front of the synagogue. But that morning was particularly difficult because of the stabbing pain in her back. She considered staying home, but desperately wanted to hear Jesus teach. There was something special about the Teacher called Jesus. Maybe He would bring the deliverance she had prayed for!

As she shuffled along to the synagogue, passersby would glance at her and then quickly look away. Over the years she had become accustomed to being invisible. Though she told herself it did not matter, her heart was familiar with the pain of feeling insignificant.

By the time she arrived, the synagogue was full and the voice of one teaching beckoned her inside. There was something unique about the tone of His voice. Being severely crippled, it was difficult to look up, but she lifted her head up with all the strength she could muster. She desperately wanted to see His face because He spoke with such strength and compassion. She was grateful that people opened up a path and she moved toward the front.

What was that? Why were people looking at her? The crowd seemed to part, leaving an open pathway to the Teacher. Was He speaking to her? Yes! She heard the question again, more clearly this time. He was asking *her* to come forward, to come to Him! He had singled *her* out! Confused, she moved toward Him and strained all the more to look into His face. Their eyes briefly met before she had to drop her head to relieve the ache in her neck.

In what ways do you relate to this disabled woman?

How was this woman marginalized, judged or overlooked due to her deformity and imperfection?

How do you think she felt regarding her beauty?

Are you in physical pain or discomfort?

Are you discouraged, depressed or weighed down by an oppressive life?

Have you suffered an injustice, as a result of evil human nature, that has kept you bound or powerless?

Do you express a resignation toward your reality? Or, even though suffering, do you live with sustaining hope?

Face-To-Face With Jesus

While Jesus was teaching, He had been aware of the shifting audience making a path for someone progressing toward the front. Turning His head, He saw a woman bended over two stabilizing canes. It took Him one look to assess her condition. Though the crippling of her body was obvious to all, only He had the ability to determine the severity of the spirit that had bound her.

In an instant He understood the depth of her multifaceted suffering. His empathy for this woman motivated Him to act. He understood the full range of emotions that accompany a physical disability and He yearned to give her rest by releasing her from the bondage she had endured for so long.

What stirs in your heart when you read about the empathy Jesus had for this woman?

Do you believe that Jesus has the same empathy for *you*?

Relative to your current situation in life, what does Jesus see when He looks into your heart?

Are you frequently disheartened by physical pain?

Do you feel emotionally beleaguered and overwhelmed?

How does your desire to be beautiful play a role in your emotions?

Have you ever felt despair or uselessness that is suffocating?

Does it take every ounce of physical strength just to continue on, even when you know your heart has been left behind long ago?

Don't throw me aside when I am old; don't desert me when my strength is gone. Psalm 71:9 CEV

 **Do any of these thoughts sound familiar to you?**

I'm not worthy of a miracle.
This is just the way it is, my lot in life.
I guess it's not that big of a deal.
I don't trust God. He never comes through for me.
I'm afraid to trust and be disappointed or hurt again.
I'm invisible.
I don't matter to anyone.
Life is too hard.
I don't have the strength to carry on.
I'm ugly.
I'm so tired of fighting this battle.
No one understands my pain.
Life's not fair.
God, why did You do this to me?
I think God enjoys watching me suffer.
I'm so angry with God.
I don't get you, God.
Haven't I suffered long enough?
Miracles only happen to others.
I'm neglected and forgotten about by others.
I get excluded and left out.

 **If any of these statements resonate with you, why do you feel that way?**

Everyone calls me a nobody. Psalm 119:141 CEV

Many are saying of me, "God will not deliver him." Psalm 3:2 NIV

Are you suffering with spiritual battles or carry unresolved bitterness?

Are you aware that an evil spirit can instigate negative thoughts such as doubt, discouragement and depression?

Do you need to be reminded that these debilitating thoughts are not from God — because His Spirit produces love, joy and peace? Even though these are real human thoughts and feelings, they do not reflect the reality of God's heart toward you.

Have you asked Jesus to shield your heart from negativity?

Don't hide Your face from Your servant, for I am in distress. Answer me quickly! Draw near to me and redeem me. Psalm 69:17-18 HCSB

Do you long for a physical healing, an emotional restoration or maybe both?

Describe what you want to be released or delivered from — a physical challenge, discouraging relationship issues or financial woes?

Do you believe that healing and restoration come from Jesus? Are you learning to rely more completely on Him for wholeness?

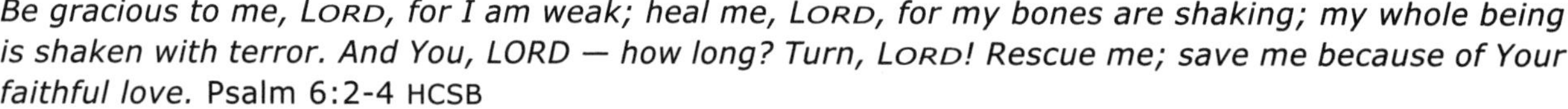

Be gracious to me, Lord, for I am weak; heal me, Lord, for my bones are shaking; my whole being is shaken with terror. And You, LORD — how long? Turn, Lord! Rescue me; save me because of Your faithful love. Psalm 6:2-4 HCSB

Arise, Lord! Deliver me, my God! Psalm 3:7 NIV

How do you continue to pursue God even during distressing situations?

What motivates you to keep moving toward God?

Are there specific Biblical passages you turn to for encouragement and hope?

Where do you hear messages of the hope, deliverance and salvation we have in Jesus?

What effort does it take for you to meet with followers of Jesus? How much of a priority is it for you? Explain.

Have mercy on me, my God, have mercy on me, for in you my soul takes refuge. I will take refuge in the shadow of your wings until the disaster has passed. Psalm 57:1 NIV

Do you believe Jesus is aware of your circumstances and that He desires to rescue and restore you?

How do you react when you read stories of miracles?

Do you think Jesus only helps "good" or "important" people?

Have your trials drawn you closer to God, or do you feel distance has increased because of your disappointment in His apparent lack of action on your behalf?

How do you react when the God who *can* rescue — doesn't?

Keep me free from the trap that is set for me, for you are my refuge. Into your hands I commit my spirit; deliver me, LORD, my faithful God. Psalm 31:4-5 NIV

Have you accepted your reality and learned to be content, regardless of your situation?

If you have not been restored or rescued, are you able to remain faithfully focused on a future time of complete deliverance?

With what level of intensity do you look forward to a future resurrection when your temporal and frail body will be restored?

In keeping with Your faithful love, hear my voice. Lord, give me life in keeping with Your justice. Psalm 119:149 HCSB

Are others bolstered in their faith by watching how you handle suffering?

If you live with frailty, how are you able to draw strength and courage from Jesus?

Are you willing to continue your pursuit of Jesus even when life is not turning out like you had hoped or planned?

Do you understand that God has the bigger picture in mind, and eventually the answer will be apparent?

May your unfailing love be with us, Lord, even as we put our hope in you. Psalm 33:22 NIV

How do you hold on to hope?

How long are you willing to wait for Jesus' answer?

Where do you see yourself in the larger story of eternity? Explain how an enlarged perspective gives you hope to continue through your trials.

What story is God writing for you, even while you wait (as this woman did eighteen years) for deliverance or a miracle?

I am certain that I will see the LORD's goodness in the land of the living. Wait for the LORD; be courageous and let your heart be strong. Wait for the LORD. Psalm 27:13-14 HCSB

We wait in hope for the LORD; he is our help and our shield. In him our hearts rejoice, for we trust in his holy name. Psalm 33:20-21 NIV

What does your heart want to say face-to-face to Jesus?

Words Spoken To The Heart

Jesus stepped toward her. With the words, "Woman, you are set free!" and the touch of His hands, she stood upright for the first time in eighteen years.

Her canes dropped to the floor. She straightened up her body, raised her arms into the air and proclaimed, "I'm free! Praise God, I'm free!" She was unaware of the scowl on the face of the synagogue ruler because she was absorbed by the impact of this miraculous event. Spontaneously she knelt down in reverence, then sprang up and grasped the hands of Jesus. Looking up into His eyes, she would always remember the look on His face. His wide grin conveyed an expression of radiant joy that she had never seen before. After giving Him a grateful hug, her feet could not contain themselves and she danced several steps with Him.

She heard the synagogue ruler begin to speak, so she backed away from Jesus, continuing to glorify God. The synagogue ruler was indignant that Jesus had healed on the Sabbath. "Hypocrites!" Jesus proclaimed. Shouldn't this woman, a daughter of Abraham, be loosed from the bondage that Satan had imposed for "*eighteen long years*"? Had He previously seen her in the community and waited for this precise time to heal her, underscoring the supremacy of love as fulfillment of the intent of the Law? Did this statement also demonstrate His divine ability to know at every moment all the details of our lives?

Regardless of the specifics that we are not aware of, Jesus' response was in keeping with His compassionate character. Jesus was undeniably pleased to liberate this woman from the evil spirit that had kept her in physical and emotional bondage for too many years. This woman who was made in God's own image was valued in God's eyes. There should be no waiting to relieve a person from suffering. Jesus had said, "Come to Me, all of you who are weary and burdened, and I will give you rest" (Matthew 11:28 HCSB). What better way to demonstrate the intent of the Sabbath rest than to give this woman rest from her suffering.

"Woman, you are set free." Luke 13:12 NIV

How do you sense these words from Jesus affected this woman physically and emotionally?

Do you ache to have the words *"you are set free"* spoken to you?

What do you desire to be "set free" from?

Do you desire release from bitterness or resentment?

"The thief comes only to steal and kill and destroy; I have come that they may have life, and have it to the full." John 10:10 NIV

Who or what is "the thief" that is working against God's will for your life? How has the thief oppressed you?

How has this thief been shown to be in contrast, and in opposition to, the life-giving and life-restoring purpose of Jesus?

Are you actively and consciously guarding yourself against "thieves"? Do you ask Jesus for protection from spiritual, emotional and physical assaults and to keep you vigilant?

"And do not bring us into temptation, but deliver us from the evil one." Matthew 6:13 HCSB

"I am not praying that You take them out of the world but that You protect them from the evil one." John 17:15 HCSB

This woman's freedom was opposed by religious leaders and humanly interpreted and legislated rules. Have you experienced opposition to your wholeness and freedom by a religion, ideology or person?

Does it surprise you that Jesus spoke against the misuse of religion because it opposed His mission of setting people free?

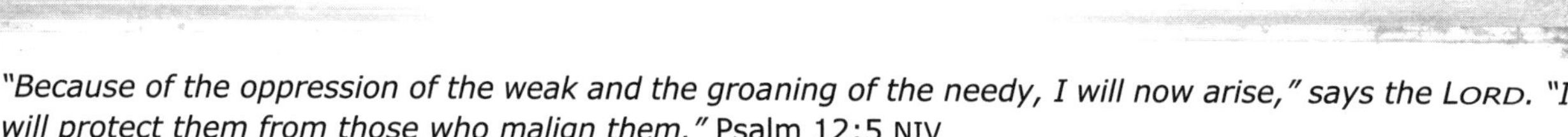

"Because of the oppression of the weak and the groaning of the needy, I will now arise," says the LORD. *"I will protect them from those who malign them."* Psalm 12:5 NIV

He said to them, "If any of you has a sheep and it falls into a pit on the Sabbath, will you not take hold of it and lift it out? How much more valuable is a person than a sheep! Therefore it is lawful to do good on the Sabbath." Matthew 12:11-12 NIV

Then Jesus said to them, "I ask you, which is lawful on the Sabbath: to do good or to do evil, to save life or to destroy it?" Luke 6:9 NIV

Jesus amazed this precious woman by releasing her from an oppressive burden. He already knew her circumstances, and it gave Him great joy to restore her!

Do you believe that Jesus is *all* about setting us free — restoring us and giving us life, if not completely during this temporal life, during a time of eternal restoration?

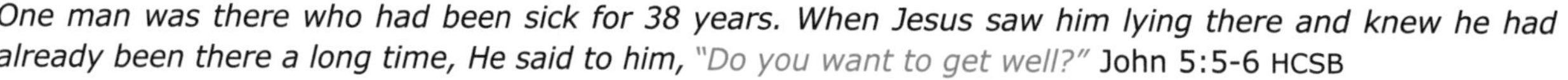

One man was there who had been sick for 38 years. When Jesus saw him lying there and knew he had already been there a long time, He said to him, "Do you want to get well?" John 5:5-6 HCSB

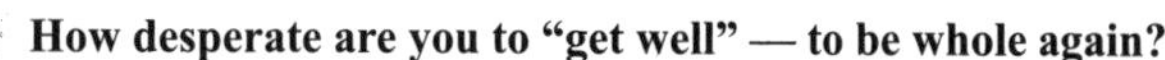

How desperate are you to "get well" — to be whole again?

Could "wellness" include more than a physical healing? Do you long for emotional and mental fortitude to gracefully handle life's inherent challenges?

Or do you want to "get well" relationally?

Though difficult, would you like to forgive someone and move forward with your life? Do you need to forgive yourself — or stop blaming God for your suffering?

A man with leprosy came to Jesus and knelt down. He begged, "You have the power to make me well, if only you wanted to." Jesus felt sorry for the man. So he put his hand on him and said, "I want to! Now you are well." Mark 1:40-41 CEV

Do you want to "get well," but are fearful of the changes that may be required?

Are you afraid that the process of restoration may be painful to endure?

God is HUGE — no task is too daunting for Him. He is Creator, sustaining the majesty and intricacies of the universe. This Jewish woman would have known the stories demonstrating His powerful ability to deliver. The Lord rescued millions of His oppressed people in Egypt and parted the Red Sea allowing escape from their Egyptian captors. The same God who delivered an entire nation of slaves from the hands of oppressors showed up to rescue and deliver *one* woman from bondage.

Does this woman's story of deliverance give you hope in His willingness and ability to rescue to *you*?

Are you encouraged to ask for and seek the restoration power of Jesus to work in *your* life?

How have Jesus' words of truth impacted your heart?

An Encounter With Jesus

This woman undoubtedly lived the rest of her days in amazement of the long-awaited deliverance that came through the actions of Jesus. She would never forget the moment when Jesus put His hands on her and she felt a surge of energy and vitality flow through her body. I would imagine her expression of gratitude was uncontainable. She not only continued to glorify God in the synagogue but also praised God while sharing the story of this miracle with all she met.

Though the news of Jesus' trial and death could have been confusing to her, maybe she understood the fulfillment of prophetic Scripture in a deeper way after His resurrection. She would have a personal understanding of the love of God who would send His Son to save His people and demonstrate the full intent of the Law.

As this blessed woman heard Scriptures read in the synagogue she probably listened to them with a new perspective. Her favorite verses had been personally fulfilled in her life, and the Messiah truly had come. Jesus, the Messiah, *her* Messiah, had come so that she could not only have spiritual life, but be able to live physically and emotionally to the fullest extent. What He had read from the book of Isaiah was true! "The Spirit of the Lord is on Me, because He has anointed Me to preach good news to the poor. He has sent Me to proclaim freedom to the captives and recovery of sight to the blind, to set free the oppressed . . ." (Luke 4:18 HCSB).

Every morning upon awakening she would consciously stretch her newly-straightened back toward the ceiling and relive that moment when Jesus set her free. This woman, a walking miracle who experienced the power of the Son of God, could show undeniable visible proof of being touched by Jesus!

What aspect(s) of God's character did this woman experience?

What stirs in your heart when you read about the compassion Jesus had for this woman?

How did Jesus restore her dignity?

I was in terrible distress but you have set me free. Psalm 4:1 CEV

He brought me out to a wide-open place; He rescued me because He delighted in me. Psalm 18:19 HCSB

How do you think she reacted to God's encounter with her?

What story would she have to share with others?

But I have trusted in Your faithful love; my heart will rejoice in Your deliverance. I will sing to the LORD because He has treated me generously. Psalm 13:5-6 HCSB

It is good to praise the LORD, to sing praise to Your name, Most High, to declare Your faithful love in the morning and Your faithfulness at night. For You have made me rejoice, LORD, by what You have done; I will shout for joy because of the works of Your hands. How magnificent are Your works, LORD, how profound Your thoughts! Psalm 92:1-2, 4-5 HCSB

Jesus saw this woman's needs, then stopped His teaching to be intentionally and fully focused, present and engaged with her.

Do you believe He has the same heart for you and wants to rescue you?

Do you long to be noticed and called out by Jesus?

Where do you need His intervention?

You are good, and You do what is good. Psalm 119:68 HCSB

Does it inspire you to know that Jesus called her — a humble woman, not a prominent person — out of the crowd?

He sees, He notices, He knows, He initiates, He calls — how do those phrases speak to your heart?

Do you believe He sees *you*, that He knows *you*?

Do you believe He desires to set *you* free? Free from what?

I will rejoice and be glad in Your faithful love because You have seen my affliction. You have known the troubles of my life and have not handed me over to the enemy. You have set my feet in a spacious place. Psalm 31:7-8 HCSB

How have you experienced God's deliverance?

Do you have a story of God's goodness that you enjoy sharing with others?

How have you been able to use your trial to demonstrate your growing faith to others?

"Go back to your home, and tell all that God has done for you." Luke 8:39 HCSB

"Go back home to your own people, and report to them how much the Lord has done for you and how He has had mercy on you." Mark 5:19 HCSB

You are kind, Lord, so good and merciful. Psalm 116:5 CEV

What would you like to say to Jesus regarding your wholeness and freedom?

Your Encounter With Jesus

Jesus, what do You want me to know about Your heart for *me*? What are You asking me to let go of?

What do You want to set *me* free from? Write what you are hearing Him say to you.

Is Jesus saying, **"You are set free"**?

My Prayer For You

Lord, you know this precious woman's name and every detail of her life, including crippling challenges, obstacles and spiritual battles. Let her know that You love her too much to leave her in a state of brokenness. Please make her profoundly aware of Your presence in her life, releasing her from any oppression or suffering she is bravely enduring. Shield her from attacks from evil spirits that attempt to thwart the joy You intend to share with her. Run after her and bolster her hope for an eternal future in Your loving grasp. Encourage her with a vision of Your desire for her restoration, wholeness and freedom. Give her Your heart's desire to set people free and provide opportunities to bring wholeness to others. I pray this in the power of Jesus' name. Amen!

Your Prayer

Thoughts Regarding Your Journey Experience

A Mother's Plea

Matthew 15:21-28, Mark 7:24-30

The intensity of a mother's love for her child can be fierce. We admire the woman in this story because of her determination to fight for the life of one of her precious babies. The passion displayed through her persistence is legendary, and Jesus' response speaks of His willingness to satisfy the desires of a mother's heart on behalf of her child. As women, our "mothering hearts" are designed to nurture and care for others in innumerable ways. We can be confident that Jesus listens to and answers our petitions that we bring to Him on behalf of those we love.

Let Your Desire Be Granted.

Through this mother's example, we can be encouraged to bring all of our desires to Jesus. Some desires may be brought out of desperation and others may include deep longings for a more complete and fulfilling life. Confidence, boldness and persistence demonstrated this woman's faith and Jesus honored her request.

In Her Shoes

Word of Jesus' power to cast out demons traveled quickly from town to town and reached a woman with a daughter who was suffering intolerably at the hand of a demon, an evil spirit. The moment she heard of this man, she determined to seek Him out, no matter the cost. She knew that Jesus was Jewish and risked being rebuffed not only because of her Gentile heritage, being an "outsider," but additionally because she was a woman. But she needed to find Him!

There is a special connection between a mother and her child. Because of that intense bond, this woman was considerably distressed to witness her daughter's agony. Nothing could be done to relieve the suffering caused by the demon. No relief was permanent, and watching the torment of her precious child was more than she could bear. Nothing was more important than to see the health of her child restored, to see her daughter once again playing happily with other children and living life as intended.

Doctors could not cure her daughter's ailment. This was a spiritual condition that she recognized could only be healed with spiritual power. The numerous accounts of Jesus' miracles were convincing. She believed that Jesus was the person who could heal her daughter. But would He help a Canaanite? And a woman, no less?

She found Jesus and began to follow Him, calling out to Him and begging Him to heal her daughter. There was no response. Out of desperation, she persisted by crying out for His attention, receiving only disdainful glances from those accompanying Him. She had nothing to lose — the only option that remained at home was the presence of an evil spirit in her child and the disgrace of being treated as social outcasts — so she continued to pursue Him. Frustrated with her insistent pleading and her incessant calls for mercy, Jesus' disciples urged Him to send her away.

Walking on, Jesus spoke to His disciples, as if ignoring her pleas. He reminded them that He was sent to the lost sheep of the house of Israel, implying that Gentiles were not the focus of His ministry. She overheard His comment but respectfully persisted, falling at His feet. "Lord, please help me!" Jesus turned and faced a woman kneeling with uplifted hands.

In what ways do you relate to this woman?

Do you empathize with this mother's fiercely devoted heart for her child and understand her act of desperation and pleading?

Have you been in a situation where you agonized over a child or a person close to you? Describe your feelings.

Have you ever been an intercessor or advocate on behalf of another? Explain.

What is your understanding of the concept of "mercy"?

Have you ever begged for mercy for yourself or for another?

Why did Jesus seemingly ignore this woman?

Do you believe that His nature is compassionate and that His actions and apparent coldness was due to a "larger story" unfolding?

Do you believe that Jesus wanted to heal this woman's daughter?

Do you believe that Jesus had the power to heal this woman's daughter?

Do you believe in your heart that Jesus is merciful and good?

Face-To-Face With Jesus

Jesus looked down to see a mother's face, strained with concern and fear over the plight of her daughter. Tear-filled eyes conveyed the depth of her distressed heart, worried only for the welfare of her child. This woman was willing to do whatever was necessary to pursue the man who she perceived was able to provide the healing relief her little child so desperately needed. This mother was not ashamed or too proud to kneel before Jesus, to beg for help and mercy on behalf of her child.

Jesus understood why a mother would risk her reputation and defy cultural standards to beg for help. He recognized the attachment that is created and solidified during a period of nine months when a woman is aware of a baby — her own child — developing inside her womb. That natural motherly bond deepens while holding her newborn to her breast and through the process of caring for her helpless, totally dependent baby.

For a mother, there is nothing more debilitating than to watch her child suffer. Perhaps for an instant, Jesus realized that in the not too distant future He would be staring into the face of another mother, His own, as she would agonize while watching her own grown child suffer. Yes, He understood.

Jesus gazed at the face of a humble woman. Humble, yet etched with uncommon determination in petitioning Him, even when ignored by Him and rebuked by those accompanying Him. As Jesus looked into her heart, He perceived a woman whose strong will conveyed trust and faith in His ability to heal and deliver her daughter from a life of despair and torment. She believed in the stories about His acts of mercy that had spread to her small town, and she trusted Him completely to extend His reputation of mercy and love to *her* child.

How does the example of this fearless mother impact you?

Do you admire her persistence?

Do you sense her complete abandonment of pride as she knelt before Jesus and begged for mercy? Are you able to be this transparent before Jesus?

Can you identify with this woman's total trust and belief in Jesus' ability to restore, heal, redeem and rescue?

When Jesus looks through your eyes, does He smile at your nurturing and committed heart for your family members and friends?

Explain a situation where you have you been continual in your petitions to God on behalf of another person.

Lord, hear my prayer; listen to my plea for mercy. Psalm 86:6 HCSB

Do you struggle with any of these thoughts or statements?

Why did God let this happen to my child?
God, are You listening to me?
God already knows the situation and hasn't answered.
I get tired of praying when I don't hear from God.
God has bigger issues than mine to be concerned about.
This request seems selfish.
I'm tired of asking God about this.
I'm not believed in or respected.

Are you able to identify the reasons why you struggle with any of these thoughts?

Lord, why do you reject me? Why do You hide Your face from me? Psalm 88:14 HCSB

Lord, do not forsake me; do not be far from me, my God. Come quickly to help me, my Lord and my Savior. Psalm 38:21-22 NIV

Are you reticent or hesitant to bring *any* issue to Jesus?

What might be holding you back — unbelief, pride, fear or mistrust?

I say to the LORD, "You are my God." Hear, LORD, my cry for mercy. Psalm 140:6 NIV

What person would you like to bring to Jesus with your mothering heart?

Are you willing to "fight" for the well-being of this person?

Describe the specific concern, whether physical, emotional or spiritual, that you are petitioning as his or her advocate.

Is there someone close to you who is engaged in a spiritual battle or suffering at the hand of an evil spirit?

Have you begged Jesus for release of this wicked spirit? Do you trust in His power to deliver?

Please listen to my prayer and my cry for help, as I lift my hands toward your holy temple. Psalm 28:2 CEV

Let all who seek You rejoice and be glad in You; let those who love Your salvation continually say, "The LORD is great!" I am afflicted and needy; the Lord thinks of me. You are my help and my deliverer; my God, do not delay. Psalm 40:16-17 HCSB

Do you feel that you do not have access to Jesus' helping hand because of your status?

Do you feel that you have to be a "religious" person for Jesus to hear your cry for help?

Do you believe that Jesus came to save ALL people?

You give hope to people everywhere on earth, even those across the sea. Psalm 65:5 CEV

Maybe you have been told or taught that it is wrong to have "desires" and that asking for even "good things" is selfish, materialistic and indulgent.

Do you consider it self-centered to ask Jesus for the "desires of your heart" such as a beautiful or safe living environment, opportunities to develop your talents, a fulfilling job, rest, new friends and avenues of exploration or adventure?

What "good thing" do you desire? Are you confident in asking Jesus for these desires of your heart?

Answer me, LORD, for Your faithful love is good; in keeping with Your great compassion, turn to me. Psalm 69:16 HCSB

The LORD is righteous in all His ways and gracious in all His acts. The LORD is near all who call out to Him, all who call out to Him with integrity. He fulfills the desires of those who fear Him; He hears their cry for help and saves them. Psalm 145:17-19 HCSB

But those who seek the LORD lack no good thing. Psalm 34:10 NIV

Is there a specific request in your personal life you would like to petition Jesus about? Please take the time to pray now from the depths of your heart.

What level of passion does this appeal stir in your heart — casual or nonchalance? Desperation or deep longing?

Do you believe God honors a passionate and zealous heart?

But as for me, LORD, my prayer to You is for a time of favor. In Your abundant, faithful love, God, answer me with Your sure salvation. Psalm 69:13 HCSB

I have sought Your favor with all my heart; be gracious to me according to Your promise. Psalm 119:58 HCSB

I call with all my heart; answer me, LORD. Psalm 119:145 HCSB

What would you like to say face-to-face to Jesus, knowing that He is listening to you?

Words Spoken To The Heart

Jesus' initial response to her request for intervention implied that she was outside His sphere of ministry. He said it wasn't right to take the food from the children of priority, the house of Israel, and give it to their pet dogs. Though the term "dog" could have been taken with offense, she remained undeterred. She maintained her composure and prepared her rebuttal. She did not give up, but pressed on with a plea of mercy in the form of a respectful argument.

Her reply was tactful, persistent and bold. She was resolute in requesting any assistance from the One she believed could heal, even if that would include "leftovers that fall from the table." She was aware that her status as a Gentile *and* a woman could have been outside of Jesus' purpose and circle of influence, but she would be grateful for even a few crumbs, not demanding or expecting anything.

It was this polite statement, conveying her faith, which elicited the answer she diligently sought. Jesus commended this Canaanite woman for her great faith and compassionately granted her heartfelt desire. Her child was instantly healed, just as she trusted would happen. Although she remains nameless in the Biblical account of her story, Jesus knew this woman's name and included her and her daughter in an eternal relationship with Him.

"Woman, you have great faith. Your request is granted." Matthew 15:28 NIV

What did those words from Jesus mean to this devoted and passionate mother?

How does Jesus' response to this desperate woman's request encourage you?

"It is not the will of your Father in heaven that one of these little ones perish." Matthew 18:14 HCSB

Do you have "great faith" to bring one of your loved ones to Jesus and surrender his or her situation to Him?

Are you willing to persist with Jesus during intercessory prayer for this person? Jesus already knows his or her needs. Could this request be used to grow your faith in God and compassion for others?

Jesus told his disciples a story about how they should keep on praying and never give up: In a town there was once a judge who didn't fear God or care about people. In that same town there was a widow who kept going to the judge and saying, "Make sure that I get fair treatment in court." For a while the judge refused to do anything. Finally, he said to himself, "Even though I don't fear God or care about people, I will help this widow because she keeps on bothering me. If I don't help her, she will wear me out." The Lord said: "Think about what that crooked judge said. Won't God protect his chosen ones who pray to him day and night? Won't he be concerned for them? He will surely hurry and help them. But when the Son of Man comes, will he find on this earth anyone with faith?" Luke 18:1-8 CEV

Jesus told his disciples: Have faith in God! If you have faith in God and don't doubt, you can tell this mountain to get up and jump into the sea, and it will. Everything you ask for in prayer will be yours, if you only have faith. Mark 11:22-24 CEV

Jesus came so that we would have "life to the full." Are there areas regarding the quality of your life that you desire to change?

Do you feel confident that Jesus approves of your bringing these longings to His attention?

Can you passionately petition for these "good things" because they seem to be aligned with God's will and purpose?

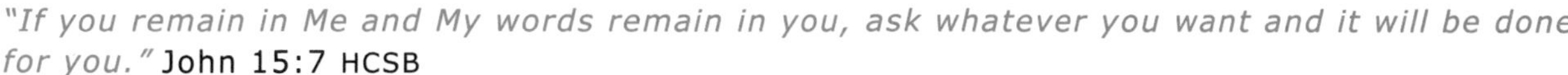

"If you remain in Me and My words remain in you, ask whatever you want and it will be done for you." John 15:7 HCSB

The phrase "your *request* is granted" is also translated "let your *desire* be granted."

Describe specific "desires of your heart." Do they include a different living environment (beautiful and safe), a new job (fulfilling and less stressful), reconciliation of family conflict, a new friend or circle of friends, a happy marriage, opportunities for personal growth, travel or service and avenues to make a difference in the lives of others?

What would that look like for you if you could have the "desires of your heart"?

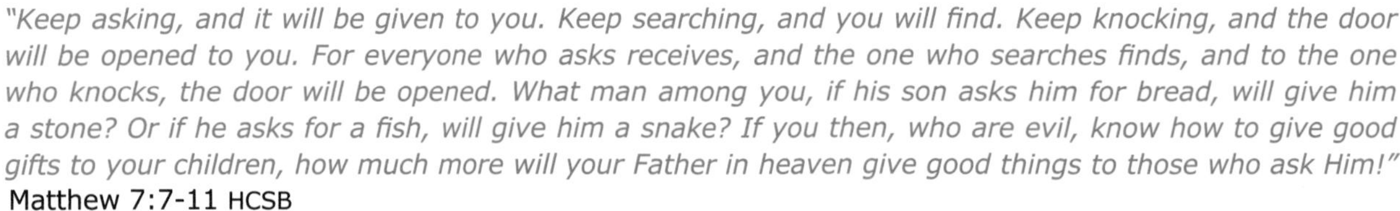

"Keep asking, and it will be given to you. Keep searching, and you will find. Keep knocking, and the door will be opened to you. For everyone who asks receives, and the one who searches finds, and to the one who knocks, the door will be opened. What man among you, if his son asks him for bread, will give him a stone? Or if he asks for a fish, will give him a snake? If you then, who are evil, know how to give good gifts to your children, how much more will your Father in heaven give good things to those who ask Him!" Matthew 7:7-11 HCSB

Then Jesus said to them, "Suppose you have a friend, and you go to him at midnight and say, 'Friend, lend me three loaves of bread; a friend of mine on a journey has come to me, and I have no food to offer him.' And suppose the one inside answers, 'Don't bother me. The door is already locked, and my children and I are in bed. I can't get up and give you anything.' I tell you, even though he will not get up and give you the bread because of friendship, yet because of your shameless audacity he will surely get up and give you as much as you need. "So I say to you: Ask and it will be given to you; seek and you will find; knock and the door will be opened to you. For everyone who asks receives; the one who seeks finds; and to the one who knocks, the door will be opened. Luke 11:5-10 NIV

Are you comfortable to "ask, seek and knock" for the desires of *your* heart, as well as on behalf of others?

Are you desperately seeking peace or joy in your life?

How would having the "desire of your heart" bring peace or joy into your life?

"Until now you have asked for nothing in My name. Ask and you will receive, that your joy may be complete." John 16:24 HCSB

What specific requests would you like to ask of Jesus? Do not hesitate, but ask confidently, passionately and persistently!

An Encounter With Jesus

After returning home, this meek, yet courageous woman found her daughter restored to health. Though not by her bedside, Jesus had healed her daughter by speaking His will. Undoubtedly, this mother would tell all who were aware of her child's condition about her conversation with Jesus and His merciful response. Surely the story would be recounted through the years, as she watched her daughter grow stronger and more beautiful, living free from suffering.

Is it possible that as she told her friends and family about her encounter with Jesus the stage was set for their foundational belief when news of His eventual death and resurrection reached their village? Would she recognize this man who she called "Son of David" as the prophesied Messiah? Would others recognize Him by remembering the story of this miracle? Maybe God would use the story of this mother — humble, tenacious and faith-filled — to bring many to believe in Jesus as Savior of *all.*

How did God reveal Himself during His encounter with this woman?

Do you have a story of a similar encounter with God — a time when you brought a loved one or situation to Jesus and He answered your plea?

Describe how this experience with God increased your faith in His goodness and faithfulness.

If a specific request has not been answered yet, are you committed to persist in prayer?

The Lord doesn't hate or despise the helpless in all of their troubles. When I cried out, he listened and did not turn away. Psalm 22:24 CEV

Lord, You have heard the desire of the humble; You will strengthen their hearts. You will listen carefully. Psalm 10:17 HCSB

How can your heart's capacity to love and care for others be expanded through tenacious pursuit of an answer from God?

Explain how your heart grows in passion toward God and devotion to others as you persist in prayer on their behalf.

I call on You, God, because You will answer me; listen closely to me; hear what I say. Psalm 17:6 HCSB

I love the LORD because He has heard my appeal for mercy. Because He has turned His ear to me, I will call [out to Him] as long as I live. Psalm 116:1-2 HCSB

Are you becoming more aware of the needs and requests of others, confidently praying on their behalf in Jesus' name?

Have you become more sensitive to meeting their needs and desires, as you are able?

Do you have a reputation as an advocate for those who are less advantaged, marginalized, oppressed by injustice or unable to speak for themselves?

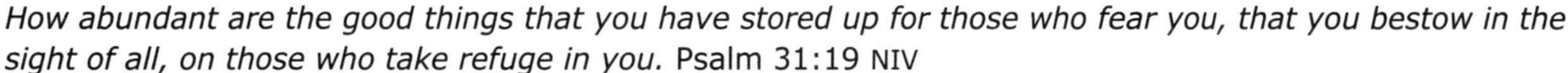

How abundant are the good things that you have stored up for those who fear you, that you bestow in the sight of all, on those who take refuge in you. Psalm 31:19 NIV

And I have said, "Only you are my Lord! Every good thing I have is a gift from you." Psalm 16:2 CEV

'But I will restore you to health and heal your wounds,' declares the LORD, 'because you are called an outcast, Zion for whom no one cares.' Jeremiah 30:17 NIV

Do you have a specific "God story," an encounter with God, when He answered a desire of your heart — either for yourself or on behalf of another?

What "good things," or gifts from God, have come as direct answer to your petitions?

What effect did that outcome have on your relationship with God?

You have granted him his heart's desire and have not withheld the request of his lips. Psalm 21:2 NIV

Trust in the LORD and do good; dwell in the land and enjoy safe pasture. Take delight in the LORD, and he will give you the desires of your heart. Psalm 37:3-4 NIV

Those who seek the LORD will praise Him. Psalm 22:26 HCSB

How does this woman's story encourage you to continue interceding in earnest and hopeful prayer as you wait for God's answer?

YOUR ENCOUNTER WITH JESUS

Jesus, what do you want me to learn from this courageous woman's story? Write what you are hearing Him say to you.

Is Jesus saying, **"You have great faith; let your desire be granted"**?

MY PRAYER FOR YOU

Heavenly Father, Giver of every good and perfect gift, only You are perfectly aware of the needs and desires of every person. Strengthen this woman's faithful and devoted heart as she relies completely on You to hear her requests on behalf of others. As she boldly seeks You out, please show Your merciful nature so that she can experience You as the divine One who listens, answers, heals, defends, protects, rescues, saves and blesses. According to Your purpose and plan, please satisfy her heart's desires as you stretch and grow her passionate and trusting heart. Give her Your loving heart for Your people, and help her to become an advocate for those who are suffering. All this is for Your glory, so that Your faithful love and compassionate power be known to all, through Jesus' name. Amen!

YOUR PRAYER

Thoughts Regarding Your Journey Experience

A Widow's Two Small Coins

Mark 12:41-44, Luke 21:1-4

The discussion of human nature would be incomplete without addressing the issue of money and its effect on people. This portrait centers on two seemingly insignificant coins and provides a lesson on value and worth — not only of money, but also of people — and challenges our attitudes toward giving. As Creator of all, what did Jesus value? This nameless widow's story has been used for centuries as an example of what is eternally important in God's eyes.

She Has Given All She Had.

In Her Shoes

Life had not been kind to her. Widowed, with no inheritance or children to support her, she faced each day as it came. This lonely woman missed her husband dearly, and though she longed for a family of her own, she was thankful that God had treated her with favor and provided for her daily needs. She knew it was by His hand that a family recently asked her to assist them with their household chores in exchange for a modest wage. After calculating that the amount earned would barely cover daily food and rent for her small living area, she praised God for His generosity towards her.

Today was special because she received not one, but two coins for finishing the family's pile of mending. After giving her employer a grateful hug, she departed their house and decided to visit the Temple on her way home. She found great peace when visiting the Temple and decided to linger today in thoughtful prayer. Firmly planted in her heart was faith that a Messiah would come with deliverance for those who were poor and oppressed. Oh, how she longed for such a time!

Surprisingly, a larger crowd than usual was milling around the grounds. She pressed towards the treasury, weaving quietly between worshippers. At times there was quite a bit of fanfare around the area where people came to place their monetary gifts into the offering box. Occasionally, an announcement was made as to the amount that an individual had deposited. She smiled to herself. Certainly no proclamation would be made about *her* offering. In fact, it was almost laughable to think that the two coins in her pocket had any significance at all.

But she had already determined to give the two small coins as an offering because of God's faithfulness towards her. Pulling the coins out of her pocket, she whispered a prayer of gratitude and dropped them in the box. She stepped away, casually looked up and caught a brief glimpse of a man seated across the way who was smiling at her. His kind look was in stark contrast to the condescending glances given when depositing her paltry contribution. Humbly, she lowered her eyes and quickly continued on her way.

How do you connect to the woman in the center of this story?

What qualities do you admire in this woman?

What was the motivation for her actions?

Can you understand this woman's willingness to give her remaining money, even though she was already extremely poor?

Have you ever felt insignificant or wanted to disappear in crowds because you felt out of place or viewed as having lesser social status?

FACE-TO-FACE WITH JESUS

Jesus and His disciples had been watching the parade of people deposit their money into the offering boxes when this woman caught His attention. What a study in contrasts! Her faded and frayed dress looked even plainer next to the fine robes of the wealthy. Additionally, her unassuming demeanor was noticeably different than those who looked self-assured about the large sums of money they had just contributed.

But it was the look in her eyes that made the loudest statement. Her unpretentious countenance reflected the pure heart of a woman who understood her status from God's perspective. Though she had lost the worldly *worth* of the status and financial security of a married woman, she understood the *true value of life* and had found contentment in widowhood. God was everything to her, and all she had left to give was her life. This woman's assurance of hope in her eternal reward translated through her serene eyes, and it made Jesus smile.

Never losing any opportunity to teach His disciples, Jesus called them closer, gesturing toward the woman He had been observing. Most likely she did not hear Jesus' words, as His response was directed to the disciples.

What does Jesus see regarding *your* worth?

Are you devalued in society's eyes because of gender, race, economic status, physical appearance, marital status or another factor? Describe when you have felt insignificant or less esteemed?

Do you think of yourself as invisible, a wallflower, believing that you have no special abilities or talents to offer, especially in comparison to others?

Have you ever felt underestimated and overlooked?

What is your honest reaction to the statement, "Jesus treasures you!"?

I am insignificant and despised, but I do not forget Your precepts. Psalm 119:141 HCSB

Do you feel that you are living in the shadow of an influential person close to you?

Is there a time when you felt that you lost your own identity as a person? Explain those circumstances and how that felt.

Do you recognize any of these thoughts as pertinent to you?

I'm invisible to others.
No one would even miss me if I were gone.
I have nothing of value to offer to anyone.
My life is so insignificant.
I'm such a loser.
Will I ever be special in someone's eyes?
God, do you even see me?
No one will remember me when I'm gone.
Compared to others, my life is so inconsequential.
No one is interested in listening to what I have to say.
What's the use? My contribution is so puny.
I am not worth anything.
No one appreciates me.
I feel useless.
I must get all I can and hang on to it.

What do you do to get "noticed"? How do you seek affirmation and attention from others?

For I am poor and needy, and my heart is wounded within me. Psalm 109:22 NIV

Hear me, Lord, and answer me, for I am poor and needy. Psalm 86:1 NIV

I am poor and needy, but, Lord God, you care about me, and you come to my rescue. Please hurry and help. Psalm 40:17 CEV

In contrast to feelings of insignificance, does Jesus see any evidence of arrogance and pride in your heart?

Have you assumed that your wealth, education, accomplishments, social standing or physical appearance increase your favor or status in God's eyes?

Can you admit to ever looking down on others who are less fortunate or poor?

Are you hesitant to befriend those who are considered to be in a lower socioeconomic level or disadvantaged?

Though difficult to admit, do you evaluate others' worth based on what they wear, their educational level, their race, their job or where they live?

Do you need to ask Jesus to help you change how you view the value of people?

Do not forget the lives of Your poor people forever. Psalm 74:19 HCSB

He determines the number of the stars and calls them each by name. Great is our Lord and mighty in power; his understanding has no limit. The Lord sustains the humble but casts the wicked to the ground. Psalm 147:4-6 NIV

What role does money play in your life? What value do you assign to money?

How is your identity connected to your monetary status?

Do you feel safer or more in control when you have money?

What are the reasons you choose to give money? Do you give to impress others?

Have you ever found yourself giving money or time unwillingly, out of duty or obligation?

Are you motivated to give with no expectation of recognition?

Would Jesus say you give humbly and with pure motives — with gratitude, purpose and joy?

It is better to live right and be poor than to be sinful and rich. Psalm 37:16 CEV

Would you like to ask God for a life of significance, an opportunity to impact the lives of others or a mission that has eternal value?

What would you like to say face-to-face to Jesus regarding human value and worth?

What heartfelt thoughts would you like to bring to Jesus regarding *your* feelings of worth?

Words Spoken To The Heart

"I tell you the truth that this poor widow has put more into the offering box than all the others." Quizzical expressions came across the disciples faces. All could see that she had only given two small coins, while many rich people were throwing in large sums.

Jesus continued, "For all of them gave out of their wealth, what they could easily spare. But she, out of her poverty, has given all she had to live on." He not only acknowledged her generosity but addressed society's standard of a person's worth. It was commonly thought that the wealthy were more favored in God's eyes, but Jesus continually put all of God's children on equal footing.

Though she was a woman, poor *and* a widow (all categories of low status in her society), Jesus made it clear that she did not have lesser value to God. She was not insignificant. In fact, by her example of sacrificial giving and sincere motives, He elevated her status, affirming the value of a pure heart.

Jesus did not condemn the rich for giving out of wealth, but emphasized the worth of one who society judged as "worthless." This woman had a heart of gold and that is what mattered. Though already poor, she still gave, not holding back anything. From a human perspective, her offering paled in comparison. But Jesus made the point that God is aware of even the smallest gift. No act of giving, and more importantly, no *person* goes unnoticed.

"She is very poor and gave everything she had." Mark 12:44 CEV

What impact do these words about this humble woman have on you?

What does it mean, she "gave everything she had"?

How do Jesus' words regarding this poor woman change how you see others?

"Blessed are you who are poor, for yours is the kingdom of God." Luke 6:20 NIV

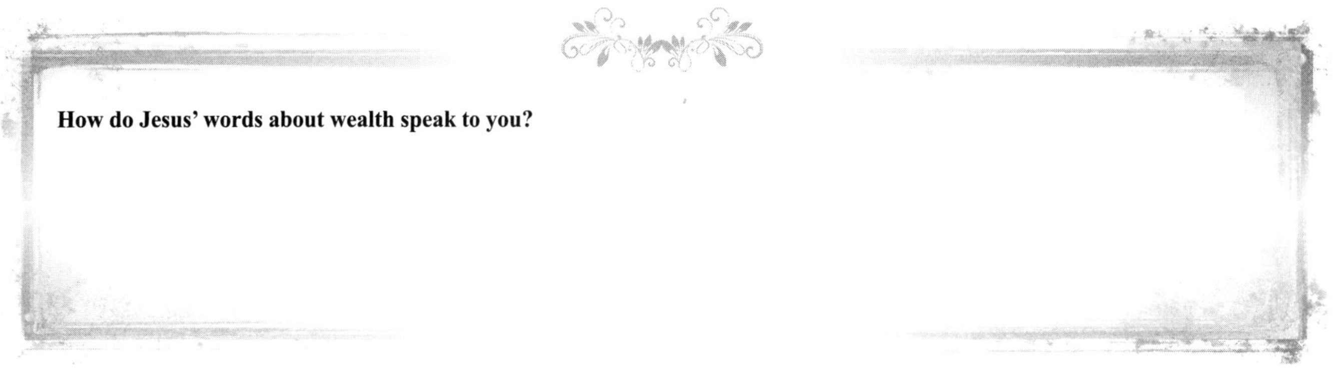

How do Jesus' words about wealth speak to you?

"Do not store up for yourselves treasures on earth, where moth and rust destroy, and where thieves break in and steal. But store up for yourselves treasures in heaven, where moth and rust do not destroy, and where thieves do not break in and steal. For where your treasure is, there your heart will be also." Matthew 6:19-21 NIV

Then Jesus said to his disciples, "Truly I tell you, it is hard for someone who is rich to enter the kingdom of heaven. Again I tell you, it is easier for a camel to go through the eye of a needle than for someone who is rich to enter the kingdom of God." Matthew 19:23-24 NIV

But Jesus told them: You are always making yourselves look good, but God sees what is in your heart. The things that most people think are important are worthless as far as God is concerned. Luke 16:15 CEV

He then told them, "Watch out and be on guard against all greed because one's life is not in the abundance of his possessions." Luke 12:15 HCSB

"Your heart will always be where your treasure is." Luke 12:34 CEV

Has your wealth affected your relationship with God?

Have you become self-sufficient instead of God-sufficient?

Do you trust in monetary security or in God's ability to provide for your daily needs?

"You say, 'I am rich; I have acquired wealth and do not need a thing.' But you do not realize that you are wretched, pitiful, poor, blind and naked." Revelation 3:17 NIV

"That's how it is with the one who stores up treasure for himself and is not rich toward God." Luke 12:21 HCSB

Has your wealth affected your passion and zeal for pursuing a relationship with God?

How much do you treasure your eternal relationship with Jesus?

Are you wholeheartedly following Jesus, or is part of your heart invested in the things and ways of this temporary world?

"No one can serve two masters. Either you will hate the one and love the other, or you will be devoted to the one and despise the other. You cannot serve both God and money." Matthew 6:24 NIV

"In the same way, those of you who do not give up everything you have cannot be my disciples." Luke 14:33 NIV

What are you thankful for?

Do you have a grateful heart for *all* the blessings in your life, even the "small" ones?

Do you intentionally express your gratitude? How?

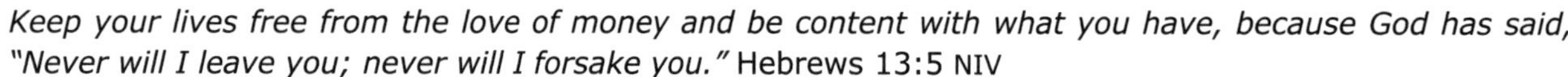

Keep your lives free from the love of money and be content with what you have, because God has said, "Never will I leave you; never will I forsake you." Hebrews 13:5 NIV

"Give us each day the food we need." Luke 11:3 CEV

Do you have a generous heart, willingly sacrificing your needs to honor God and help others with your money, time and talents?

How are you able to give God "everything you have"? Does it help to be reminded that in reality, *everything* belongs to God?

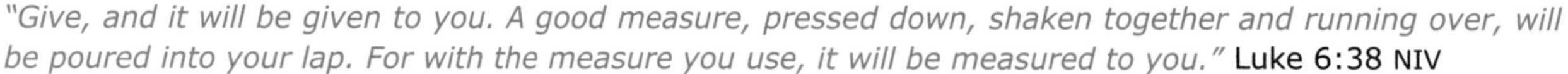

"Give, and it will be given to you. A good measure, pressed down, shaken together and running over, will be poured into your lap. For with the measure you use, it will be measured to you." Luke 6:38 NIV

"His master replied, 'Well done, good and faithful servant! You have been faithful with a few things; I will put you in charge of many things. Come and share your master's happiness!'" Matthew 25:21 NIV

"Whoever is faithful in very little is also faithful in much, and whoever is unrighteous in very little is also unrighteous in much." Luke 16:10 HCSB

Regardless of others' perspectives, do you feel that you, as a person, are valued and significant? Explain how this is possible.

Would Jesus comment on your quiet confidence as you stand respectfully in His presence?

Are you convinced that Jesus knows you and is concerned for your situation here on earth — that He loves you and will never forget or abandon you?

"For all those who exalt themselves will be humbled, and those who humble themselves will be exalted." Luke 14:11 NIV

"God blesses those people who are humble. The earth will belong to them!" Matthew 5:5 CEV

"Whichever one of you is the most humble is the greatest." Luke 9:48 CEV

Do you long to hear words from Jesus that confirm your worth in His eyes?

An Encounter With Jesus

This woman's situation did not change after this non-verbal encounter with Jesus. In fact, she was probably unaware that Jesus' comments were even made about her. She might have been embarrassed to know her example of generosity would inspire millions throughout the centuries. But she would have been pleased with Jesus' affirmation that those who are devalued, overlooked and marginalized have value in the eyes of God.

Just as with this poor widow, there may be times when you sense that humans do not value you and your life seems insignificant and useless. Maybe you are not rich, famous, beautiful, specially gifted or have societal status. But do you sense Jesus' loving glance as you humbly come to Him? As you give of yourself, even your entire life, are you assured of validation in Jesus' eyes, giving you contentment and peace? Just as this poor widow understood the true meaning of life, do you believe that temporal values will pass away? Do you place your hope in the eternal? In Jesus' eyes, you are significant, valued and loved!

Have you experienced God in such as way as to understand the value He gives to you?

Summarize your understanding of how deeply valued each person is in God's eyes.

How does the awareness of God's love for humanity affect your interaction with each individual with whom you come in contact?

Though the Lord is exalted, he looks kindly upon the lowly. Psalm 138:6 NIV

Regardless of the circumstances in your life, what do you value most?

Can you truly say that you place your value and trust in those things that have eternal worth and significance?

Do you long for the time when you will see Jesus face-to-face and hear Him say, "Well done! Your reward is in heaven!"?

Have you learned to be grateful and in a constant attitude of praise, regardless of your circumstances?

He put a new song in my mouth, a hymn of praise to our God. Many will see and fear the Lord and put their trust in him. Psalm 40:3 NIV

What have you learned from this treasured woman?

Has her example altered how you view the poor and those who are seen as "lesser" in society's eyes?

Does her story change how you see yourself in God's eyes?

Do you sense that you are always in His care?

Are you encouraged to know that Jesus sees who you uniquely are?

Regardless of how you are viewed in human eyes, do you feel as though you are irreplaceable and matter to God?

The poor can run to you because you are a fortress in times of trouble. Psalm 9:9 CEV

You, Lord, are my shepherd. I will never be in need. Psalm 23:1 CEV

How does understanding Jesus' love for the poor and those of "lesser" status alter your attitude and lifestyle?

Do you genuinely befriend those who have no ability to promote you or give to you?

Are you generous, especially to those who are in need?

The poor and the homeless won't always be forgotten and without hope. Psalm 9:18 CEV

Would you like to ask Jesus to change your viewpoint on any areas related to this portrait?

Would you like to hear affirmation regarding your status in His eyes?

Following Jesus' example, what words of affirmation and statements of value can you give to others?

Do you have any final thoughts regarding value or worth (of money or people) that you would like to bring to Jesus?

Your Encounter With Jesus

Jesus, what do You want me to learn from this humble woman's example? Write what you are hearing Him say to you.

Is He affirming your value by saying, **"She has given all she had"**?

My Prayer For You

Lord, we come into Your presence, humbled by Your greatness. Though You are powerful beyond description and imagination, please show this treasured woman that she matters to You and is of infinite worth because she was created in Your image. Pour out Your favor on her so that she has no doubt as to how precious she is to You and how much You delight in her. Please give her Your perspective on the value of each person with whom she comes in contact. Help her to see how every person, regardless of worldly worth, is deeply valued and loved in Your eyes. Provide opportunities for her to affirm the value of those who are invisible and marginalized. Help her to trust You to supply her daily needs and grow her thankfulness for Your blessings. Expand her willingness and capacity to generously give completely of herself in ways that have eternal significance. I pray these things in Your Son's name, Jesus. Amen!

Your Prayer

Thoughts Regarding Your Journey Experience

A Woman Fully Known

John 4:4-30, 39-42

"Life hadn't turned out as she had expected or planned." Can you relate to that statement? This portrait is about a woman who has more in common with us than we may initially want to admit. She tried to fill the emotional void in her heart in an attempt to drown out the nagging thoughts of futility. But on a fateful day she came face-to-face with the only One who could eternally quench her thirst for life.

I Am He.

How many of us put on our outward face in an attempt to hide our emptiness, restlessness or feelings of being lost and defeated? There is something missing, or at least our heart tells us so. But who really knows or understands our deepest thoughts and our life stories? One seemingly casual interaction with Jesus turned this woman's world around. Could it be that Jesus is the answer for you, too?

In Her Shoes

Here she was again — going through her typical routine of walking to Jacob's well to draw water. Most women arranged their trips to the well during the cool of the day, but facing the other town women was awkward. She avoided them by making her trek in the middle of the day.

The nagging ache in her heart would not go away. Life certainly had not turned out as she expected or planned. No one seemed to understand her unsettled heart and discontentment. Certainly her actions towards the town men did not help her cause. She was embarrassed to admit that she used her beauty to attract a man and yes, she *was* difficult to live with. It didn't take long for the man to leave, confirming her worthlessness and deepening her loneliness. The cycle would repeat again. This was all she could trust.

How she longed for a friend — someone to talk to who understood her and would not judge her because of her failings. She felt so hollow at times. The men in her life did not fill the hole in her heart. With each failed relationship her reputation as a desperate and desolate woman was solidified. Life was confusing and meaningless.

Women shunned her, and men took advantage of her emotional weakness. Here she was again on yet another scorching ordinary day, wishing for a fresh start or a way to undo the grief and heartache she had caused. If she could run away . . . well, she just could not bear to face anyone today.

Oh, groan, there was someone sitting by the well. A *man*. She certainly did not feel charming today. A *Jewish* man. He definitely would not speak to *her*, a Samaritan woman. Avoiding His glance, she quickly proceeded to draw water into her empty jar. Wiping the sweat from her brow, she poured water into a cup and began to take a drink.

"Please give me a drink of water." What?! She couldn't believe that this Jewish man had actually spoken to her and she looked up.

What circumstances in this woman's life made her feel empty and restless?

How do you relate to her situation or what she was feeling?

Are your relationships fulfilling? Explain your answer.

Maybe life is going relatively well for you now, but do you still hear yourself saying, "There has got to be more"? Are *you* "thirsty" for more?

Face-To-Face With Jesus

Jesus was exhausted from His travels and had stopped at Jacob's well for a drink. Even though there was great animosity between the Jews and Samaritans, Jesus chose to pass through Samaria. While resting, He watched a Samaritan woman approach. At first glance, she was an average woman going about her daily routine. But there was something unusual about this woman. She was all alone in the heat of the day, and Jesus could see that she was deep in thought and avoiding eye contact with Him.

After His request for a drink of water, she was now looking directly at Him with a look of astonishment on her face. With a skeptical tone she replied, "How can You ask *me* for a drink? You are a Jew and I am a Samaritan woman." Maybe she was slightly annoyed that yet again, a man was asking for something from her. But the tone of this man's request and the way He looked at her *was* different. Her guard was down, the mask was off and the dialogue was about to begin.

Looking through her cautious eyes, Jesus could see a restless woman who made no attempt to conceal her dissatisfied and empty heart. She was thirsty, but not necessarily for water. She was thirsty for Life, and He was the only One who could fill her dry and weary soul.

Is it easy for you to see how empty this woman is because *your* heart is empty?

What does Jesus see when He looks into *your* heart? Are you discouraged or depressed? Does your heart feel dull, without feeling, lifeless, restless or dissatisfied?

Have you experienced boredom with life or blasé mediocrity? Do you desire for escape or feel a sense of futility?

Have you ever been rejected by family or friends?

Could you be lonely, but not want to search out friends? Do you ever feel lonely, even when people are around?

Have people ever commented on your guardedness?

Do any of these statements sound familiar?

I want to escape.
I just want to run away.
I don't want to see anyone.
I'm so screwed up.
Everyone thinks I'm crazy.
No one really understands what I am feeling.
I don't care anymore.
Life isn't worth living.
Nothing matters anymore.
No one wants me around.
There's got to be more to life than this.
I'm such a mess.
Life is meaningless.
If anyone really knew who I am, they wouldn't like me and I'd be all alone.
It's no wonder no one loves me.
I'm depressed.
I just wish that someone would know and love ME.
I'm such a failure.
I can't get anything right.
I always get put down.
I'm not enough.
I'm too much.

Why am I so depressed? Why this turmoil within me? Psalm 42:5 HCSB

Have there been times in your life that you have felt "empty"? What did or does that look like?

Do you feel that life is incomplete, purposeless or joyless? Can you explain the reason for this void?

Are you tempted to fill the hole in your heart — this emptiness — with substitutes and addictions, such as overeating, smoking, alcohol, drugs or excessive shopping?

Do you fill your time with busyness, hobbies, service, searching the internet, watching TV, online networking or other ways in an attempt to silence the nagging restlessness?

Have you found yourself trying to escape your seemingly meaningless and boring life by watching the lives of others on "reality" shows or following the culture of "celebrity"?

Are you consumed with the illusive pursuit of beauty and youthfulness?

Have you become a workaholic and highly driven in search of a sense of fulfillment?

I wish I had wings like a dove, so I could fly far away and be at peace. I would go and live in some distant desert. I would quickly find shelter from howling winds and raging storms. Psalm 55:6-8 CEV

Have you attempted to satisfy a thirsty heart with relationships, either by seeking the affection from sexual partners or by trying to win approval from others?

What has been the result of your attempts to silence the messages of an empty heart?

Do you feel out of sync with God's will in your life? Explain how that has impacted the relationships closest to you.

Could it be that self-dependence plays a role in dissatisfaction with life? Explain how that might apply to you.

God, You are my God; I eagerly seek You. I thirst for You; my body faints for You in a land that is dry, desolate, and without water. Psalm 63:1 HCSB

Are you trying to run away from something — an uncomfortable circumstance or consequence of sin in your life?

Are you running from God, trying to avoid His glance? What are you trying to hide from Him?

What are you embarrassed for others to know about you? Are you afraid that people will reject you if they know who you really are or what you have done in the past?

Are you afraid that Jesus will reject you, too?

Do you believe Jesus sees the beauty within you?

Is there anything you feel afraid to tell Jesus or share with Him?

Does the example of this woman make you realize that though fully known, Jesus treats you with respect and loves you unconditionally, overlooking your mistakes?

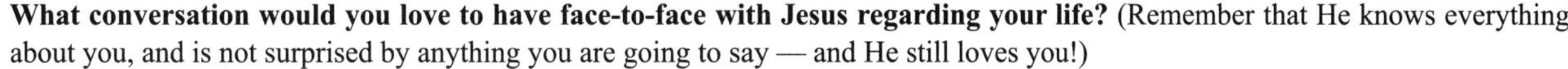

As a deer gets thirsty for streams of water, I truly am thirsty for you, my God. In my heart, I am thirsty for you, the living God. When will I see your face? Psalm 42:1-2 CEV

What conversation would you love to have face-to-face with Jesus regarding your life? (Remember that He knows everything about you, and is not surprised by anything you are going to say — and He still loves you!)

Words Spoken To The Heart

With a unique twist of the conversation, Jesus said that if she knew God's gift, that is Who was asking for a drink, then she would have asked *Him* and *He* would have given her *living water*. She was intrigued about this living water and asked Him to give her this water so she would not get thirsty and have to keep coming back for more. Jesus had her attention and now told her, "Go, call your husband and come back." He knew this was her heart's soft spot — that of unfulfilled love and loss. Relationally, she was continually thirsty, but never satisfied.

With downcast eyes she quietly replied, "I have no husband." Without hesitation, He confirmed that she was right. "You've had five husbands and you're not married to the man you're living with now!" She was shocked! How could He have known about her personal life? Who *was* this man?

"Sir, I can see that You are a prophet." She changed the subject to that of religion, contrasting where the Samaritans and "you people," the Jews, worship. But Jesus pointed out that there was a time coming — actually it was there now — when true believers will be led by the Spirit to worship in truth, hinting that God was reconciling both groups, the Samaritans and Jews, and making Himself accessible to all.

Her face brightened and with deep conviction of expressed hope the woman stated, "I know that Messiah is coming, and when He comes, He will tell us everything." All the unanswered questions she had about life would be explained when the Messiah she longed for came.

"I, the person speaking to you, am He." Jesus said it! He chose to reveal Himself as Messiah to this outcast Gentile woman. Momentarily, her face was frozen in an expression of awe, wonder and puzzlement. When the disciples arrived, they were surprised to find Jesus talking with a woman, but did not interrupt to question Him because they could sense the intimacy of the conversation. Though we are not privy to the remaining dialogue, the effect of Jesus' encounter with this Samaritan woman was profound.

"I, the one speaking to you — I am he." John 4:26 NIV

How did the pronouncement that Jesus is the Messiah impact this woman?

What do those words mean to you?

Why does it matter that Jesus is the Messiah? What difference does that make in *your* life?

"If anyone is thirsty, he should come to Me and drink! The one who believes in Me, as the Scripture has said, will have streams of living water will flow from deep within him." John 7:37-38 HCSB

Have you been looking for the Messiah to save you?

How do you desire to be saved? What from?

Are you looking to Jesus to help you overcome an addiction?

Are you ready to release control over your life, your fears, guilt, anger and resentment to Him?

Do you see that Jesus' invitation to life can fill the void in your heart? Instead of looking for relief through futile physical substitutions and addictions, *He* is the source of fulfillment.

Would you like to be closer to Jesus, but do not know how to make that happen?

Then Jesus declared, "I am the bread of life. Whoever comes to me will never go hungry, and whoever believes in me will never be thirsty." John 6:35 NIV

"Blessed are those who hunger and thirst for righteousness, for they will be filled." Matthew 5:6 NIV

He said to me: "It is done. I am the Alpha and the Omega, the Beginning and the End. To the thirsty I will give water without cost from the spring of the water of life." Revelation 21:6 NIV

Have you been searching for the Messiah to satisfy your thirst and give life? Describe where that search has taken you.

Do you believe that though Jesus fully knows you, He still has accepted you, desires a one-on-one relationship with you and is pursuing you?

Can you see that Jesus is totally present and available for you?

Do you believe that Jesus was sent to give *you* life — eternal life?

Have you heard His invitation and believe His words of truth?

Have you accepted His gift of living water, which is eternal life?

"I assure you: Anyone who hears My word and believes Him who sent Me has eternal life and will not come under judgment but has passed from death to life." John 5:24 HCSB

"What exactly does God want us to do?" the people asked. Jesus answered, "God wants you to have faith in the one he sent." John 6:28-29 CEV

What would you like to say to Jesus regarding your thirst or emptiness?

AN ENCOUNTER WITH JESUS

Suddenly, trivial matters, such as drawing water were unimportant. Leaving her water jar behind, she hurried back to town to share what had just happened. "Come and see a man who told me everything I have ever done! Could it be that this is the Messiah?" His ability to look into her heart and fully understand her life convinced her that this man could be the Anointed One, the Christ! Jesus Himself even declared that He was the One!

Jesus had miraculously opened her eyes to see that He alone had the answers to her questions and simultaneously provided the solution to her misdirected longings. Previously, her quest to understand the mysteries of life had sent her down a path that left her feeling shallow and unfulfilled. But one encounter with Jesus transformed her. Life was no longer meaningless. She now had new perspective — an eternal perspective.

What was so persuasive about this woman's story that influenced the town people to make their way toward Jesus? Maybe it was because her countenance had changed. Her eyes danced with joy and a smile filled her face! Surprisingly, there was new passion in her voice. The issues that had consumed her were no longer of concern. She was settled and her heart was overflowing with joy. She was whole, restored and fully alive! Life had clarity. This marginalized woman was suddenly different, and the people were intrigued by this remarkable transformation. So out of curiosity, they came to see the man she was so excited about.

The encounter with the woman at the well revealed that Jesus, the Messiah, is the One who gives living water and eternal life. The Samaritan woman persuasively told others this good news about Jesus, encouraging them to "come and see" for themselves. And because of *one* woman sharing her personal experience, many of the Samaritans also believed He was the Messiah, the one called Christ, the Savior of the world.

How did the Samaritan woman experience God?

Have you had a similar encounter when you met the Messiah?

What is your reaction to the knowledge that Jesus is the only One who knows every detail of your life, yet He continues to love you?

Does that convince *you* that He is the Messiah?

Have you experienced God as the Living Water who quenches the thirsty void in your life? If so, explain.

God, Your faithful love is so valuable that people take refuge in the shadow of Your wings. They are filled from the abundance of Your house; You let them drink from Your refreshing stream, for with You is life's fountain. Psalm 36:7-9 HCSB

Describe how meeting Jesus has impacted and changed your life.

Do you have a new zest for life, empowered by Jesus' love for you?

Does your life have new or renewed purpose?

Have those close to you noticed a difference in your countenance after encountering Jesus?

I proclaim righteousness in the great assembly; see, I do not keep my mouth closed — as You know, LORD. I did not hide Your righteousness in my heart; I spoke about Your faithfulness and salvation; I did not conceal Your constant love and truth from the great assembly. Psalm 40:9-10 HCSB

For who in the skies can compare with the LORD? Who among the heavenly beings is like the LORD? Psalm 89:6 HCSB

Can you relate to how excited this woman was to tell everyone about her encounter with Jesus?

Can you confidently proclaim that Jesus is the Messiah, the One sent to restore, save and give life?

Do you feel compelled to share with others how you have experienced God's goodness in your life — how He knows you personally and filled your emptiness?

How have you encouraged others to "come and see" Jesus?

Come and see the works of God; His acts toward mankind are awe-inspiring. Psalm 66:5 HCSB

Your Encounter With Jesus

Jesus, what are You trying to teach me through this woman's story? Write what you are hearing Him say to you.

Is Jesus saying, **"I am He"**?

My Prayer For You

Lord, we come to You empty and thirsty, depleted by the cares and futility of this world. Forgive us for attempts to satisfy our restless and broken hearts by shallow acts of desperation. Instead, help us understand the depths to which You fully know us, yet continue to love and pursue us. Please let this woman experience Your grace, quenching her thirst for life by meeting and knowing You! May she bask in the wonder of how You can personally know *her*, the details of *her* life's journey and the plans that You have for *her*. Give her confident hope in eternal life that only comes from You, the Messiah. Empower her with an uncontainable urge to bring others to meet You. Let all those she comes in contact with be impacted by her contagious awe of Your goodness. In Jesus' name, who makes this possible, I pray. Amen!

Your Prayer

Thoughts Regarding Your Journey Experience

A Merciful Rescue

John 8:2-11

Sex. That one word seems to get everyone's attention because of the significant role affection and physical intimacy plays in human relationships. In this portrait we meet a woman who has found herself in the center of controversy because of a sexual act she committed that was opposed to society's moral law.

Has No One Condemned You?

What is the intended purpose of sex? How do sin, obedience, guilt and condemnation enter the picture? With only a few words, Jesus addressed these questions and resolved an inflammatory situation, leaving no doubt as to His divine ability to judge fairly, while holding this woman accountable for her actions.

In Her Shoes

With eyes closed, one can almost hear the commotion created as the group of men ran toward Jesus with a disheveled woman in tow. She struggled to maintain her balance as she was pushed by those around her. A crowd was gathering, running alongside to witness the inevitable confrontation. Eager for a quick display of justice, they hurled accusations at her while they hustled toward the Temple. Undoubtedly, Jesus heard the uproar and was aware of the developing scene as they approached His seated position.

Shoving her toward Jesus, they called His name. He looked up to see a frightened woman who was grasping the clothes that had been hurriedly put on after being caught in the act of adultery. Her tear-filled eyes were cast to the ground. The reality of her situation was overwhelming, and she was overcome with humiliation and helplessness. Well aware of the consequences of her sin, she shuddered at the thought of facing the expected judgment.

Trying to disguise their motives, the religious leaders phrased their question to Jesus, "In our Law, Moses commanded that such a woman be stoned to death. What do *You* say?"

Jesus saw through the veil of their righteous indignation and into their hypocritical and conniving hearts. The accusers had callously exploited this woman by using her as bait to trap Him. They were more concerned with exposing Jesus as a fraud than with *her* as a person. Their double standard of morality was also apparent as they were quick to charge a woman for adultery, yet her adulterous male partner was nowhere to be seen. In essence, these men could not see that her obvious lack of morality matched their own.

Refraining from looking at those questioning Him, Jesus calmly began writing something in the dirt. The woman was holding her breath, her very life dependent upon His response. The noisy crowd quieted. All were waiting for His answer.

Jesus stood up and gave a penetrating look at each of her accusers. Then He spoke in a commanding, yet gracious tone, "The one of you who is without sin, let him be the first to throw a stone at her." Without another word, Jesus bent down and continued to write in the dust.

This challenging statement delivered a conviction of unconfessed sin. Each person present was forced to recognize not only his own sinfulness, but the possibility that this man might truly be the Son of God. The woman watched with relief as one by one, the men left the scene — an acknowledgement of their own sin. She was left alone with Jesus. "What would He do to her?" she wondered.

Jesus stood up and faced the woman.

In what ways do you connect with this woman?

What do you think led this woman into the arms of a man other than her husband?

What is your understanding regarding sexual relations outside of marriage?

Have you ever been "caught in the act" or been legitimately guilty of wrongdoing?

Can you recall a time when you faced dire consequences because of your improper or illegal actions?

With what tone does Jesus address the accusers?

What was the intent of Jesus' statement to the accusers?

How would you describe the difference between "guilt" and "condemnation"?

Face-To-Face With Jesus

Jesus looked into eyes filled with tears that reflected a heart aching from guilt, shame and hopelessness. Only He could perfectly understand the reason why this woman was involved in an illegal relationship. Was she seeking love from someone other than her husband because she was in a marriage that was loveless or abusive? Had she been tossed out of a marriage by a heartless husband without a proper bill of divorcement that allowed her to legally remarry? Did she seek the attention of another man because he provided financial or emotional support? Even within this illicit relationship, had she been exploited for political gain by her lover? Had her emotional vulnerability been used to her partner's advantage?

No matter the reason, Jesus saw standing in front of Him a desperate woman who had lost her way and was living outside of God's will for her life. She was pursuing love and acceptance, but from a relationship other than the one God had originally intended — a marriage that was bound by covenant.

Can you empathize with this woman's feelings of shame, embarrassment and panic?

Have you ever faced a situation where you "hit the bottom," were doomed, with no hope in sight?

Are you presently experiencing "guilt," knowing that you have done something wrong?

Do you still feel accepted and loved by Jesus?

What does Jesus see when He looks into *your* heart?

I am faint and severely crushed; I groan because of the anguish of my heart. Psalm 38:8 HCSB

Feelings of guilt are appropriate because they indicate recognition of doing something wrong. When you hurt someone or sin against God, your conscience nags at your heart with a conviction that you have gone against God's will. Hopefully, your heart regrets the actions and seeks forgiveness, prompting you to confess your sin to God and the person you hurt.

Would not God have discovered it, since he knows the secrets of the heart? Psalm 44:21 NIV

My guilt has overwhelmed me like a burden too heavy to bear. Psalm 38:4 NIV

Are you currently feeling pangs of guilt because you have sinned against another person?

Are you carrying guilt because a wrong choice or mistake has reaped negative consequences?

Or maybe you are feeling guilty for a "secret" sin, afraid that others will find out about the "true you."

Do you see that all sin is essentially going against God, in opposition to His will?

I said, "Have mercy on me, Lord; heal me, for I have sinned against you." Psalm 41:4 NIV

Do you carry guilt because you are living or have lived in a sexually impure relationship or situation?

Are you searching for love to fill an empty heart because you are insecure or lonely?

Would you admit to being "needy" of a man's attention and affection?

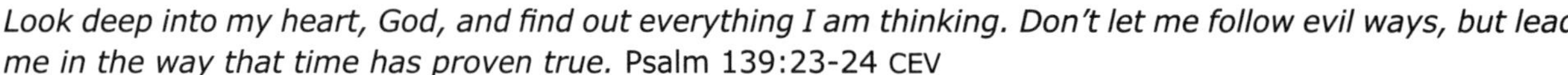

Look deep into my heart, God, and find out everything I am thinking. Don't let me follow evil ways, but lead me in the way that time has proven true. Psalm 139:23-24 CEV

How does your beauty play a role in your relationship with men?

Do you feel compelled to alter your body to attract a man?

Is your beauty the foundation of your relationships?

Feeling guilty is different than self-condemnation. Guilt says, "I did something wrong." Shame and self-loathing says, "I *am* something wrong." Have you experienced a time when your guilty heart turned to self-condemnation?

Have you ever entertained any of these condemnatory thoughts?

I blew it and God's turned His back on me.
God will never forgive me for what I've done.
I'm no good.
God doesn't love me anymore.
I'm worthless.
I'll have to try harder to be good.
I'm so ashamed I want to hide.
I'm such a disappointment.
My sin is too big to forgive.
My sins are too many to forgive.
I am hopelessly flawed.
I want to go to sleep and never wake up.
Why would God rescue me when I got what I deserved?
I got myself into this mess. I guess I'll have to get myself out of it.
God wants me to burn in hell.
I hate myself.
I'm tired of being pushed around and forced into things.
I don't get treated fairly.

Have you allowed your negative emotions to become a habitual way of thinking?

The Lord is close to the brokenhearted and saves those who are crushed in spirit. Psalm 34:18 NIV

You are my King and my God. Answer my cry for help because I pray to you. Psalm 5:2 CEV

In what way(s) do you long for redemption and deliverance in your life?

How do you long for a Savior?

Are there areas in your life that are out of sync with Jesus' will for your life?

What sins and guilt would you like to surrender at His feet?

Be gracious to me, God, according to Your faithful love; according to Your abundant compassion, blot out my rebellion. Wash away my guilt, and cleanse me from my sin. For I am conscious of my rebellion, and my sin is always before me. Against You — You alone — I have sinned and done this evil in Your sight. Psalm 51:1-4 HCSB

Are you in a situation where you need a "rescue"? Explain.

Remember that "rescue" does not mean that the consequences of sin will be removed. However, a rescued sinner can rest assured that she is forgiven and can walk a new path.

Are you seeking a rescue from a negative situation that you are partially or completely responsible for (such as this woman)?

Have you ever blamed God for consequences that you caused? Do you expect or demand that He fixes your humanly-caused problems?

What happens when He doesn't rescue you from circumstances that have been caused by human missteps?

Would you like a fresh start, a second chance? What would that look like for you? How would that make you feel?

I patiently waited, LORD, for you to hear my prayer. You listened and pulled me from a lonely pit full of mud and mire. You let me stand on a rock with my feet firm, and you gave me a new song, a song of praise to you. Many will see this, and they will honor and trust you, the LORD God. Psalm 40:1-3 CEV

"Call on Me in a day of trouble; I will rescue you, and you will honor Me." Psalm 50:15 HCSB

On the day I called, You answered me; You increased strength within me. Psalm 138:3 HCSB

Could it be that you need a rescue from enemies or someone who intends to harm you?

Maybe you are enduring a situation where you are mistreated because you are a follower of Jesus. Is this currently the case?

Save with Your right hand and answer me so that those You love may be rescued. Psalm 108:6 HCSB

But I trust in You, LORD; I say, "You are my God." The course of my life is in Your power; deliver me from the power of my enemies and from my persecutors. Psalm 31:14-15 HCSB

Are you standing before Jesus "condemned" in the eyes of others right now? Describe how that feels.

Who are your accusers?

Return to your rest, my soul, for the LORD has been good to you. For You, [LORD,] rescued me from death, my eyes from tears, my feet from stumbling. I will walk before the LORD in the land of the living. Psalm 116:7-9 HCSB

The LORD will rescue his servants; no one who takes refuge in him will be condemned. Psalm 34:22 NIV

Turn, LORD! Rescue me; save me because of Your faithful love. Psalm 6:4 HCSB

What would you like to say face-to-face to Jesus regarding any guilt or condemnation you are burdened with? Will you ask Him to take away your heaviness of heart and give you peace?

Words Spoken To The Heart

"Where are they? Has no one condemned you?" In contrast to the harshness she had been previously subjected to, Jesus treated her with dignity. She acknowledged that no man remained.

"Then neither do I condemn you," He replied. "Go and sin no more."

Jesus did not condemn her, but He also did not *condone* her sinful actions. Instead, He challenged her to a lifestyle change — commanding her to leave her life of sin that would never satisfy her lonely heart. Pursuing an adulterous affair was not God's will for her ultimate happiness. His compassionate act of redemption emphasized that anything outside of God's intent could never bring fulfillment, only guilt and negative consequences.

By His merciful response, this woman had just experienced the psalmist's statement, "He will not always accuse . . . He does not treat us as our sins deserve" (Psalm 103:9-10 NIV).

"Has no one condemned you?"

"Then neither do I condemn you," Jesus declared. *"Go now and leave your life of sin."* John 8:11 NIV

In what ways would this woman have been affected by her encounter with Jesus? Describe the impact Jesus' words had on her.

How do those same words from Jesus speak to *your* heart?

How liberating is it to know that Jesus does not condemn *you*? Explain how this truth changes your perception of God.

"For God so loved the world that he gave his one and only Son, that whoever believes in him shall not perish but have eternal life. For God did not send his Son into the world to condemn the world, but to save the world through him." John 3:16-17 NIV

If Jesus has forgiven you and does not condemn you, why do you allow self-condemnatory thoughts to linger in your heart?

Are those messages from God or from Satan, the master deceiver and accuser?

Have you grown up with a religious tradition of an angry God eager to send sinners to hell? How do the words of Jesus oppose that view?

Do you truly believe that Jesus was sent by His Father in heaven to *save* the world, not *condemn* it?

Do you truly believe that Jesus was sent to *save* you, not *condemn* you?

"No one who has faith in God's Son will be condemned. But everyone who doesn't have faith in him has already been condemned for not having faith in God's only Son." John 3:18 CEV

God is angry against sin — not the sinner. He is angry against sin because His nature is holy, perfect and righteous, and sin opposes God. Because God knew that we humans are *not* holy, but broken and flawed, He sent His son, Jesus — the Holy One — to save *all* sinners. He did this out of His love — for *you*!

"I tell you the truth, whoever hears my word and believes him who sent me has eternal life and will not be condemned; he has crossed over from death to life." John 5:24 NIV

Do the words "leave your life of sin" pierce and convict your heart in any way? (Remember that guilt is appropriate if there is sin in your life, but self-condemnation and doubt of God's love is not.)

What would you like to say to Jesus regarding any guilt or self-condemnation you may be burdened with?

Are there areas in your life that you are convicted to change?

Do you understand that the Holy Spirit was sent to act as Counselor, guiding you toward God's will for your life?

"Nevertheless, I am telling you the truth. It is for your benefit that I go away, because if I don't go away the Counselor will not come to you. If I go, I will send Him to you. When He comes, He will convict the world about sin, righteousness, and judgment." John 16:7-8 HCSB

This portrait specifically addressed the topic of sexual relations and confirms that extramarital sex (sex outside of covenanted marriage) is not according to His will, and therefore, sin.

What are your thoughts regarding His words on the original design and purpose of marriage?

"Haven't you read," he replied, *"that at the beginning the Creator 'made them male and female,' and said, 'For this reason a man will leave his father and mother and be united to his wife, and the two will become one flesh'?"* Matthew 19:4-5 NIV

Would you agree that sex, the act and intimacy of "one flesh," is intended only for husband and wife?

Would that imply that sexual purity is defined within the context of a covenant relationship between a man and woman?

Can you see how Jesus has your best interests at heart by protecting the institution of marriage through sexual purity?

Explain the intended benefits of a sexual relationship only within the context of marriage.

"But in the beginning God made a man and a woman. That's why a man leaves his father and mother and gets married." Mark 10:6-7 CEV

What is God's intent for your sex life?

Are you willing to trust that living within His will for your sexuality is for your benefit and ultimately a blessing?

Have you experienced any negative consequences because of premarital or extramarital sex?

What is the most difficult aspect of remaining committed to sexual purity?

Do you believe that Jesus will help you live a life of purity?

Would you like to ask Jesus to purify your life right now?

"For the Son of Man came to seek and to save the lost." Luke 19:10 NIV

Just as this woman was "lost" and was rescued by Jesus, we have hope that no matter how "lost" we are, He desires to save us. The Holy Spirit brings an awareness of sin to our hearts, convicting, but not condemning us. We recognize we are living a life of sin and are not in alignment with God's will. We bring our confession, along with a repentant heart, and receive Jesus' loving forgiveness. Our guilt is gone, and with a pure heart we stand face-to-face with Jesus, looking to Him and His words to guide us through life according to His will.

"What do you think? If a man owns a hundred sheep, and one of them wanders away, will he not leave the ninety-nine on the hills and go to look for the one that wandered off? And if he finds it, I tell you the truth, he is happier about that one sheep than about the ninety-nine that did not wander off. In the same way your Father in heaven is not willing that any of these little ones should be lost." Matthew 18:12-14 NIV

Once rescued from condemnation, we are challenged to leave a life of sin and to live in obedience by following Jesus.

Do you resist the word "obedience" and the surrender that it requires?

What does it take to follow and obey Jesus?

"If you love me, keep my commands." John 14:15 NIV

He said to him, "Love the Lord your God with all your heart, with all your soul, and with all your mind." Matthew 22:37 HCSB

"Whoever wants to be my disciple must deny themselves and take up their cross and follow me." Mark 8:34 NIV

What does it mean to "deny" yourself? Could this mean to deny yourself the proclivity to do what *you* want regarding the way you live?

Do you make your own rules regarding your lifestyle (maybe based on what society says is acceptable) — essentially picking and choosing the aspects of following Jesus that are comfortable for you?

"And whoever doesn't take up his cross and follow Me is not worthy of Me." Matthew 10:38 HCSB

"My sheep hear My voice, I know them, and they follow Me." John 10:27 HCSB

One way to follow Jesus is to imitate the way He mercifully treats people. Do you have the tendency to judge people?

Has someone sinned against you and "deserves" punishment? Can you offer mercy to that person, as Jesus did?

Are you able to forgive an individual when that person hurts you?

"Do not judge, and you will not be judged. Do not condemn, and you will not be condemned. Forgive, and you will be forgiven." Luke 6:37 NIV

"You hypocrite, first take the plank out of your own eye, and then you will see clearly to remove the speck from your brother's eye." Matthew 7:5 NIV

"Be merciful, just as your Father is merciful." Luke 6:36 NIV

How do you learn about God's will? Where would you find His teachings and words?

What is the result of following Jesus?

What are the consequences of living in God's will for your life?

Then Jesus spoke to them again: "I am the light of the world. Anyone who follows Me will never walk in the darkness but will have the light of life." John 8:12 HCSB

Do you see how important it is to rely on words of truth to change your way of thinking and living?

Do your thoughts, emotions and actions reflect words of truth?

Describe the areas of your heart or life you would like to surrender to His merciful and loving nature.

 **What requests regarding "rescue" would you like to present to Jesus?**

An Encounter With Jesus

What relief! She didn't immediately rush away, but lingered, taking in the reality of her situation. Who was this man who had rescued her? There was something different about Him. Though not condoning her sinful action, He seemed to understand her plight as a woman. Treated with contempt by other men, Jesus showed her respect. Judged and condemned by other men, Jesus showered her with redemptive mercy and grace.

I wonder how this redeemed woman would have responded. Maybe she was initially too stunned to react. Did she later seek Jesus out to express her thankfulness? Would she watch Jesus from a distance as He taught the masses and eventually become one of His followers? Did their eyes ever meet again? Would she witness the upcoming events when Jesus was subjected to unjust condemnation from a crowd?

What would it have been like for her to be legally condemned by religious leaders seeking justice for a sinful action, and then rescued from imminent execution? Could she sense that Jesus saw her human value and loveliness? This man perceived her lonely heart, accepted her as a person, yet challenged her to live a life of holiness. The impact on her life must have been profound!

Even though her guilt most assuredly was mercifully erased by forgiveness, this woman's situation may not have changed. In fact, she may have faced additional adversity as a consequence of the sin and public disgrace of being an unfaithful wife. Maybe her husband would divorce her. Most likely, this woman's reputation was forever tainted. Would her former accusers retaliate in another way because they were thwarted in their attempt to trap Jesus?

No matter what she endured the rest of her life as a result of sinful choices, undoubtedly she would cherish this encounter with a man who treated her with undeserved compassion and rescued her from punishment, a death sentence. One would hope this woman lived with an acute appreciation of Jesus' loving forgiveness and therefore, carefully and respectfully walked a path that reflected her gratitude for this remarkable act of redemption when guilt and condemnation were released, and she was given a second chance to live untarnished in God' eyes.

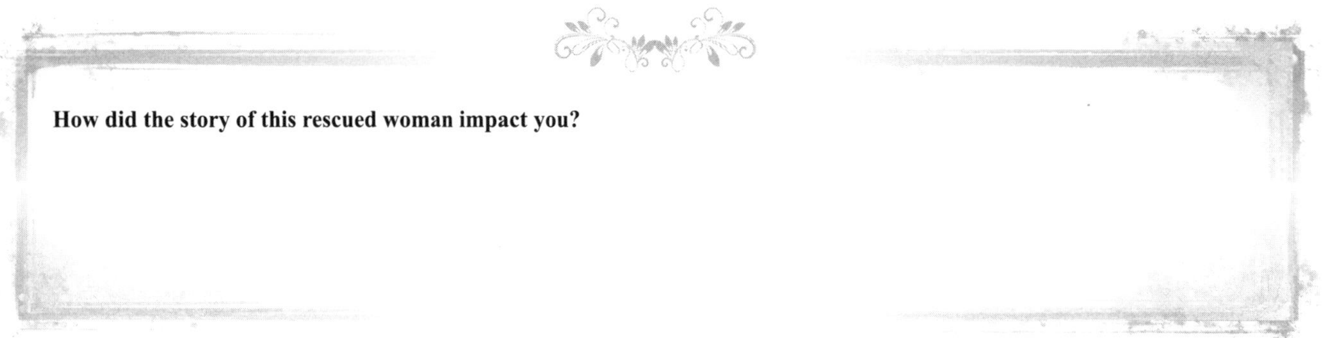

How did the story of this rescued woman impact you?

Our God is a God who saves; from the Sovereign Lord comes escape from death. Psalm 68:20 NIV

What characteristics of God did this redeemed woman experience?

You are merciful, Lord! You are kind and patient and always loving. Psalm 145:8 CEV

But you, Lord, are a compassionate and gracious God, slow to anger, abounding in love and faithfulness. Psalm 86:15 NIV

He loves righteousness and justice; the earth is full of the Lord's unfailing love. Psalm 33:5 HCSB

You are my mighty rock, my fortress, my protector, the rock where I am safe, my shield, my powerful weapon, and my place of shelter. Psalm 18:2 CEV

How have you experienced God's undeserved kindness — His mercy? Are you discerning His loving presence in your life?

Following Jesus' example, are you able to see people with non-condemnatory eyes and treat them with undeserved kindness, mercy and love?

We praise you, Lord God! You treat us with kindness day after day, and you rescue us. Psalm 68:19 CEV

I trust your love, and I feel like celebrating because you rescued me. You have been good to me, Lord, and I will sing about you. Psalm 13:5-6 CEV

My eyes are always on the Lord, for He will pull my feet out of the net. Psalm 25:15 HCSB

What is the outcome of being rescued by Jesus?

Do you think this woman treated her rescue casually, or do you think her encounter with Jesus transformed her life?

But I live with integrity; redeem me and be gracious to me. Psalm 26:11 HCSB

May the words of my mouth and the meditation of my heart be acceptable to You, Lord, my rock and my Redeemer. Psalm 19:14 HCSB

Do you think this woman lived with the same intense awareness of her rescue ten years later?

Could she have forgotten the impact on her life and fallen back into familiar and self-directed patterns of living? Do you think she could have taken for granted the mercy that was extended to her?

How do you keep your relationship with Jesus vibrant, fresh and growing, even after many years elapse from your first encounter with Him?

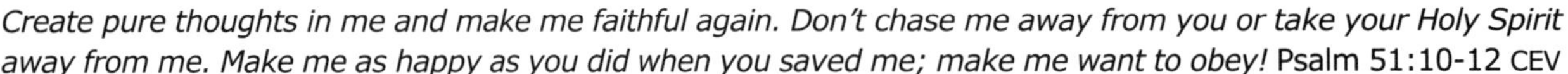

Create pure thoughts in me and make me faithful again. Don't chase me away from you or take your Holy Spirit away from me. Make me as happy as you did when you saved me; make me want to obey! Psalm 51:10-12 CEV

Keep your eyes on the Lord! You will shine like the sun and never blush with shame. Psalm 34:5 CEV

What would you like to say to Jesus, your Redeemer?

Your Encounter With Jesus

Jesus, what do You want me to understand about You through this woman's story? Write what you are hearing Him say.

Do you hear Jesus asking, **"Has no one condemned you?"**

Do you hear Jesus saying, **"Go and leave your life of sin"**?

My Prayer For You

Father, You designed us to be relational, sexual and emotional beings. Sadly, sometimes the created qualities You called "good" are misdirected and our lifestyle choices reap consequences that cause heartache and grief. Please give this woman wisdom to discern Your intention for the relationships in her life and discipline to run from situations that are not of Your will. Come to her rescue as she seeks Your involvement in her life. And as she desires, bless her with a loving marriage that reflects Your intended purpose for the unity of a man and woman.

Lord, release this woman from any shame and guilt she carries and let her feel Your unlimited forgiveness that frees her to walk blamelessly with You. Rescue her from any brokenness as she surrenders her failed attempts at life into Your capable hands. When she acknowledges her desperation and incompleteness, draw her to You and help her to see that You are her only hope. Compel her to follow in Your footsteps, treating others with mercy and forgiveness. In Jesus' name, I pray. Amen.

Your Prayer

Thoughts Regarding Your Journey Experience

Martha's Belief In The Messiah

John 11:1-7, 17-45

Who is Jesus? Martha knew Him as her friend and acknowledged Him as the Son of God. But Jesus had so much more to teach her about who He was. Martha's understanding that "God is God — and we are not" deepened after a revelation of His mysterious nature and power that defied human logic. She learned to surrender her expectations of God and her inclination to manage and control life by completely trusting in Jesus, the Messiah and her Lord.

I Am The Resurrection And The Life.

In Her Shoes

One of Jesus' friends, Lazarus, suddenly became ill. His sisters, Martha and Mary, were also close friends and had spent numerous hours visiting with Jesus when He was in Bethany. There was no hesitation about sending word to Jesus concerning Lazarus' illness because they had already witnessed His miraculous healing power and assumed that He would immediately return to restore their brother.

But Jesus had other plans. Though He was aware of Lazarus' illness and the distress of His friends, He lingered. He followed the will of His Father, knowing God's glory would be revealed through the events He would orchestrate.

"Where could Jesus be? Why hasn't He responded? Surely He knows how desperately we need Him now!" Martha and Mary struggled to trust Jesus and fought against disappointment, but continued to anticipate His arrival. Lazarus progressively grew weaker. He quickly succumbed and was buried. Martha and Mary were crushed and in shock. Not only had they lost their brother, but now they had doubts about Jesus. Why hadn't He come?

Many friends and family were gathered at Martha's and Mary's house to comfort the sisters. A visitor burst through the door announcing, "Jesus is on His way!" Immediately, Martha wrapped a shawl around her head and hurried out to greet Him. Looking down the path, she searched the faces of those approaching. There He was! Though weary from grief, she brightened with relief when she saw Him.

Rushing toward Him, she blurted out, "Lord, if You had been here, my brother would not have died." Then she respectfully added, "But even now I know that God will give You whatever You ask."

How do you relate to Martha and Mary in their time of distress?

Have you ever been faced with a situation that forced you to ask the question, "Where is God?" Describe how that challenged your faith.

Have you ever been frustrated by Jesus' silence?

Have you ever been disappointed with Jesus, thinking that He let you down?

When have you doubted that Jesus would come through for you?

How have those doubts or disappointments impacted your relationship with Him?

Has there been a challenge in life that you felt you could not endure?

Have you ever panicked in a situation because you felt you were losing control?

Do you want to trust God, but find it difficult to see beyond your "obvious" reality?

Face-To-Face With Jesus

Dear Martha — such a faithful friend. He, along with many others, had been the recipient of her gift of hospitality, as she was well known for her competent ability to organize events. Now, looking through her eyes, He could see the complex mix of emotions — grief and hope, doubt and trust, assertiveness and reliance, impatience and faith, confusion and deference. Jesus loved how her natural tendencies toward management had mellowed after His reminder about priorities. He also knew how difficult it was for her to relinquish control and patiently trust Him.

It deeply moved Jesus to see the pain in Martha's eyes. Lazarus was dead and His cherished friends were overcome with sorrow. Their belief in Jesus had grown during their friendship, but now it was being tested. They could not see beyond their narrow, human viewpoint.

Do you feel a personal connection to Martha and understand what Jesus saw in His friend?

Can you relate to Martha's ability to share her authentic thoughts and feelings with Jesus?

Do you feel comfortable asking Jesus for help in such an intensely passionate manner as Martha?

What does Jesus see when He looks into *your* heart during a trial?

Day and night my tears are my only food, as everyone keeps asking, "Where is your God?" Psalm 42:3 CEV

Have you ever felt defeated or abandoned, yet hung on to hope, wanting desperately to believe that God would arrive on the scene?

Has God ever given an answer or response you did not understand?

Has there been a time when God said "no" to a prayer and you walked away from Him?

Do you have the proclivity to take control of your life? Describe how you react when you feel you have no control over a situation.

Is your personality more laid back, with a "whatever will be, will be," even fatalistic, attitude?

Could it be that you've lost faith in God's ability to hear and answer your prayers?

I am worn out calling for help; my throat is parched. My eyes fail, looking for my God. Psalm 69:3 NIV

Which of the following phrases sound familiar?

This looks impossible.
I don't see any way out.
Can I trust God?
Why hasn't He responded?
I'm at my wit's end.
Why did God let this happen to me?
I can't take this anymore!
I don't think that God is involved in my life.
I'm starting to lose control.
Why doesn't God fix this?
I don't get any help. I have to take care of myself.
I'm not sure God is going to come through for me.
God, where are You?

Listen to my prayer, O God, do not ignore my plea; hear me and answer me. My thoughts trouble me and I am distraught. Psalm 55:1-2 NIV

Are you comfortable approaching Jesus as one of His friends?

Or do you have reticence about bringing a request to Jesus?

Do you doubt His ability to hear and answer your prayers?

Is your trust in Jesus being challenged right now? Can you explain how?

Pay attention to the sound of my cry, my King and my God, for I pray to You. At daybreak, LORD, You hear my voice; at daybreak I plead my case to You and watch expectantly. Psalm 5:2-3 HCSB

What doubts would you like to share face-to-face with Jesus?

Words Spoken To The Heart

Jesus gave Martha a comforting embrace and said reassuringly, "Your brother will rise again." Yes, Martha believed that Lazarus would rise again at the Resurrection in the future. In her mind though, that still did not take away her present confusion of Jesus' actions or deep pain from the loss of her brother.

Jesus spoke again, "I am the resurrection and the life! Whoever puts his trust in Me will live, even though he dies; and everyone living and trusting in Me will never die. Do you believe this?"

"Yes, Lord, I believe that You are the Messiah, the Son of God, the One who was to come into the world." Martha's statement of faith affirmed she believed with all of her heart that Jesus was the prophesied Messiah and had the authority to give eternal life. But the reality still remained — Lazarus was dead. Would Jesus do something in *this* life, or in the one to come?

"I am the resurrection and the life!" John 11:25 NIV

How have you experienced the reality of Jesus at this point in your spiritual journey?

Do you believe Jesus is God? Describe how you have personally confirmed your belief in Him.

What does the statement "Jesus is Messiah" mean to you?

While he was still speaking, suddenly a bright cloud covered them, and a voice from the cloud said: This is My beloved Son. I take delight in Him. Listen to Him! Matthew 17:5 HCSB

And a voice from heaven said, "This is my Son, whom I love; with him I am well pleased." Matthew 3:17 NIV

"But what about you?" he asked. "Who do you say I am?" Luke 9:20 NIV

Do you agree that God determined at the beginning of time to send His only Son, Jesus, to redeem all humanity from our sinful nature?

Do you believe that Jesus was sent to save you — to reconcile you back to God, forgiving your sins and offering you eternal life, instead of death?

What physical realities still limit your belief in God's power? Explain any difficulty you have with seeing beyond your present reality.

Do you recognize Jesus' sovereignty over all things, including the universe and life itself?

Can you say with conviction, "Jesus, You are the Messiah!"?

"This is eternal life: that they may know You, the only true God, and the One You have sent —Jesus Christ." John 17:3 HCSB

"For this is the will of My Father: that everyone who sees the Son and believes in Him may have eternal life, and I will raise him up on the last day." John 6:40 HCSB

"I tell you for certain that the time will come, and it is already here, when all of the dead will hear the voice of the Son of God. And those who listen to it will live! The Father has the power to give life, and he has given that same power to the Son." John 5:25-26 CEV

Have you taken the next step to declare, "Jesus, You are Lord of my life — I trust You!"?

Do you trust that Jesus has your best interests at heart?

Will you trust Jesus to answer your prayers according to His will, timing and eternal perspective?

"Do you believe that I am able to do this?" Matthew 9:28 NIV

Then Jesus said, "Did I not tell you that if you believe, you will see the glory of God"? John 11:40 NIV

What situation are you currently struggling to surrender in faith to Jesus?

How have you placed God in a box, with limited expectations of His ability to answer your needs?

Have you attempted to manipulate God in an attempt to get the answer you want? Explain.

So then he told them plainly, "Lazarus is dead, and for your sake I am glad I was not there, so that you may believe." John 11:14-15 NIV

Are you willing to completely trust in His timing, as He works out the details of your "larger" — and eternal — story?

Are you asking for Him to expand your view of His "bigness"?

Are you willing to be surprised by Him and His response?

"If you love me, you will do what I have said, and my Father will love you. I will also love you and show you what I am like." John 14:21 CEV

Have you committed to following Jesus by wholeheartedly trusting in His involvement in your life?

Do you trust that whatever Jesus does is for your eternal benefit and will bring glory to God?

Jesus replied, "Anyone who loves me will obey my teaching. My Father will love them, and we will come to them and make our home with them." John 14:23 NIV

"I have called you friends, because I have made known to you everything I have heard from My Father." John 15:15 HCSB

What would you like to say to Jesus, your Friend?

An Encounter With Jesus

Martha went back into the house where her distraught sister Mary was being consoled by friends. When Mary was told Jesus was asking to see her, she quickly left the house. When she saw Him, she too told Jesus, "Lord, if You had been here, my brother would not have died." Mary also trusted in His healing power and assumed that had He been there, Lazarus would have been healed. But it was clear Jesus had not come through as both expected.

"Where have you buried him?" Jesus calmly asked. "Come and see," they replied. Then they led Him to the tomb, weeping as they walked. It pained Jesus to see how heartbroken His friends were and how human perspective limited their belief. He too wept. His love for His friends was undeniable to observers, though many also questioned why Jesus allowed Lazarus to die.

What happened next turned the world upside down, not only for those witnessing the event, but for those who would hear the story repeated. When Jesus asked Martha to take away the stone, she resisted, knowing that Lazarus had been dead four days and the body would stink. But Jesus gently reminded her that if she would keep trusting, she would see the glory of God. So the stone to Lazarus' grave was removed and the crowd quieted down, hands placed over their noses in anticipation. No odor! Quizzical looks covered faces, then all eyes turned to Jesus.

Jesus offered up a brief prayer so those present would believe He had been sent by His heavenly Father. Then, with the words "Lazarus, come out!" the unthinkable happened. The man, previously dead for four days, walked out of the tomb with strips of burial linen wrapped around his body. Those in the crowd stared in disbelief, initially stunned into silence. "Unwrap him!" Lazarus was unveiled and then spontaneous and boisterous praise began! Martha and Mary rushed to give Lazarus hugs, their tears of joy flowing freely.

The dramatic intervention in the lives of Jesus' closest friends started the commotion that eventually led to His arrest. He certainly must have known that this display of divine power would unleash a fury of opposition, but He would not have had it any other way, for this was the plan. Jesus chose His friends as the recipients of this blessing and miracle of restored life, and He willingly sacrificed His safety because of His tender love for them. As a result, many would believe He was the Messiah.

Martha had learned to surrender her proclivity to control and arrange her life by completely depending on Jesus, trusting in His power and on His timing. Truly, the timing of this amazing miracle was perfect! Jesus' timing is *always* perfect, orchestrated to bring glory to His heavenly Father.

One would assume that Martha, Mary and Lazarus would be among the most ardent and vocal witnesses to the divinity of Jesus, as they personally experienced His undeniable power — the power to heal, to restore and to resurrect. They would testify that without a doubt, Jesus *is* the Resurrection and the Life!

How big is your view of God? Do you desire that your understanding of who God is — who Jesus is — be deepened?

Jesus is the GREAT "I AM" revealed from the beginning of time and throughout the pages of the Bible! His thoughts, plans and power are bigger than our most competent human ability to imagine or describe. He sees the divine picture and has perfect timing in addressing our needs. And when He rescues or answers our requests, our understanding of His "bigness" grows, and we can praise Him with a fresh perspective of His glory.

God IS, because He IS — He doesn't have to define, explain or justify Himself. He is God! Perfect, Holy, Righteous, Unfailing, Everlasting and Ever-present! "I AM BECAUSE I AM" (Exodus 3:14). Humans will never be able to completely understand Him or His actions. He's mysterious and unpredictable — He's God and we are not! But we can stand in awe, believe and trust.

*Jesus answered, "You are from below, but **I am from above**. You belong to this world, but I don't. That is why I said you will die with your sins unforgiven. If you don't have faith in me for who **I am**, you will die, and your sins will not be forgiven."* John 8:23-24 CEV

*"So why do you accuse me of a terrible sin for saying that **I am** the **Son of God**? After all, it is the Father who prepared me for this work. He is also the one who sent me into the world."* John 10:36 CEV

*Jesus answered, "You are right in saying **I am a king**. In fact, for this reason I was born, and for this I came into the world, to testify to the truth. Everyone on the side of truth listens to me."* John 18:37 NIV

*"You call me **'Teacher'** and **'Lord'**, and rightly so, for that is what **I am**."* John 13:13 NIV

*"**I am** the **living bread** that came down from heaven. If anyone eats of this bread he will live forever."* John 6:51 HCSB

*"**I am** the **true vine**, and my Father is the gardener."* John 15:1 NIV

*"**I am** the **light of the world**. Whoever follows me will never walk in darkness, but will have the light of life."* John 8:12 NIV

*"**I am** the **good shepherd**. The good shepherd lays down his life for the sheep."* John 10:11 NIV

*"**I am** the **way**, the **truth**, and the **life**. No one comes to the Father except through Me."* John 14:6 HCSB

*"**I am** the **door**. If anyone enters by Me, he will be saved and will come in and go out and find pasture."* John 10:9 HCSB

*"**I am Jesus**."* John 18:5 CEV

*"**I am** the **Alpha** and the **Omega**," says the Lord God, "who is, and who was, and who is to come, the Almighty."* Revelation 1:8 NIV

How have you experienced the Great "I AM" in your life?

Describe the specific aspects of His nature you have been introduced to during your journey with Jesus.

Let me experience Your faithful love in the morning, for I trust in You. Reveal to me the way I should go, because I long for You. Psalm 143:8 HCSB

"Be still, and know that I am God; I will be exalted among the nations, I will be exalted in the earth." Psalm 46:10 NIV

How difficult is it to surrender your fears, impatience and proclivity to control to God — even to an Almighty, All-powerful God?

Does it help knowing that you are entrusting your life and circumstances to the Son of God, the Messiah, THE Lord of the universe?

The Lord does whatever He pleases in heaven and on earth, in the seas and all the depths. Psalm 135:6 HCSB

The Lord is my strength and my shield; my heart trusts in Him, and I am helped. Therefore my heart rejoices, and I praise Him with my song. Psalm 28:7 HCSB

Only God knows your future and has the power to be your Shield and Strength — either protecting you from a situation or giving you strength to walk through it. Are you ready to relinquish the striving to control your life and give it totally to Jesus?

Are you ready to completely trust in Jesus, THE Messiah?

Say to my soul, "I am your salvation." Psalm 35:3 NIV

Be still before the Lord and wait patiently for him; do not fret when people succeed in their ways, when they carry out their wicked schemes. Psalm 37:7 NIV

Yet He saved them because of His name, to make His power known. Psalm 106:8 HCSB

Does Martha's story increase your perspective of God's guiding hand in your life?

How does Martha's story encourage you to share a "bigger" viewpoint of God with others?

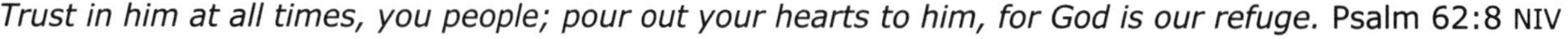

Trust in him at all times, you people; pour out your hearts to him, for God is our refuge. Psalm 62:8 NIV

What would you like to say to your Friend, *your* Lord, THE Messiah?

Your Encounter With Jesus

Jesus, what more do You want me to know about You? Write what you are hearing Him say.

How is Jesus saying to you, **"I am the resurrection and the life"**?

My Prayer For You

Lord, come to this woman and show her Your saving power. Allow her to see You as the Son of God, the Messiah, erasing any lingering unbelief. Open her ears and heart to hear Your voice of truth that demonstrates who You are. Settle her down with Your calming presence and cause her to be still while she expectantly waits for Your perfect will and timing to work in her life. Increase her trust in You, Creator and Sustainer of the universe, and in Your mysterious nature. Encourage her with glimpses of how her life fits into the "larger story" of eternity. With Your words, speak life into her.

And when this woman undeniably experiences Your hand in her life, let her give You all the credit and glory for amazing her with Your unfailing love. As You enlarge Yourself in her heart, provide opportunities for her to tell others about You — the All-powerful, All-knowing, Ever-present, Everlasting Father and Eternal Lord of the universe. All this I pray in Jesus' name, The Great I AM! Amen!

Your Prayer

Thoughts Regarding Your Journey Experience

Mary's Expression Of Devotion

Matthew 26:6-13, Mark 14:3-9, John 12:1-8

Although this encounter took place centuries ago, the woman at the center of the story has been remembered because of her extravagant and unrestrained adoration of Jesus. If Mary were alive today, she would be able to describe what it means to "have a relationship with Jesus" because she had the privilege of interacting with Him on numerous occasions and was one of His closest friends. What does an intimate relationship with Jesus look like? How does the recipient of His love naturally relate to Him? Mary of Bethany's beautiful example enlightens and inspires us.

She Has Done A Beautiful Thing For Me.

We are given a glimpse into Mary's life by observing an unabashed and public demonstration of her devotion to Jesus. Mary had no doubts as to who Jesus was and that He loved her. Jesus' response to her worship affirmed His delight in our expression of gratitude for the incalculable role He plays in our lives, as Savior and Redeemer.

In Her Shoes

A dinner in Jesus' honor was held after Lazarus was raised from the dead, and though the religious leaders were known to be actively seeking His arrest, Jesus' friends courageously gathered. Mary was especially excited to see Jesus, as she always looked forward to listening to what He had to say. Honestly, it was more than just listening to His words and teachings — she loved being with *Him*. She wanted to drink in every nuance of His tone, His thinking and His feelings. She wanted to know Him *completely*, including His message of life and truth, His purpose — and His heart.

From the moment Mary saw Jesus step through the door, she sensed a change in His demeanor, but she was not quite sure how to describe it. She had witnessed the varied nature of His personality — lighthearted, even playful, serious, joyful and authoritative. Most recently, He had shown the tender empathy of a friend when she was grieving.

Because she had spent so much time studying Jesus, her intuition told her something was different about Him. Was it a heaviness of heart? A foreboding mood? Was He contemplative? It was not sorrow, but was it turmoil? His disposition was not directed inward — it could never be said that Jesus was focused inward. In fact, He seemed to want to linger and be with His friends, clearly enjoying their company.

But Mary sensed that He would be leaving soon. Though she did not completely understand it, there was something unsettling about the nature of His recent messages. Where was He going? Reflecting on His words, random thoughts popped in her head . . . something would be required of Him . . . of her . . . sacrifice, death, resurrection, life. Maybe she was just recalling the amazing events surrounding Lazarus' death and restoration to life. No, there was definitely an ominous feeling at this gathering.

Oh, how she loved this man, this Son of God. But not in a typical human sense. Yes, He was her friend, but so much more. Jesus was her Teacher, Master and Lord. He meant everything to her. She desired to demonstrate her devotion, but how could she possibly express the depths of her heart? Of course — she knew exactly what she wanted to do!

After ensuring that Martha had all the preparations under control, Mary slipped out the door and hurried home. Sitting on a shelf was a decorative jar made from alabaster. This bottle of precious perfume had been given to her and she had been saving it for a special occasion. Mary tenderly picked it up and held it to her nose, hoping for a whiff of the fragrance captured inside.

Mary returned with her prized possession and as she entered the door, all eyes turned to her. The dinner had already begun, and Martha served the meal while Lazarus, Jesus and His disciples were seated around the table. It only took one look at the elaborately decorated jar in her hands for all to recognize that it held expensive perfume. Impulsive and emotional Mary . . . what was she up to? Though Mary was known to be demonstrative, they certainly did not expect what happened next.

Mary struck the neck of the jar against the table, releasing a powerful scent. She approached Jesus and without a word poured the contents of the *entire* bottle on His head and feet, the potent aroma filling the house. And then, with an expression of humility and devotion to her Lord, Mary kneeled before Him and began wiping His feet with her hair.

The guests were astonished at this outlandish demonstration and the disciples started grumbling angrily. Oh, to be sure, the culture required anointing the head of a guest with oil, washing his feet and giving a kiss, but wasn't this overdoing it? The grumbling intensified to harsh rebuke with the men chastising Mary, not for being scandalous, but for being wasteful. Judas was the strongest objector. "The perfume is worth a year's wages! It could have been sold and the money given to the poor!"

Though Mary was not concerned about their opinions, she hesitated momentarily, concerned that her actions were ill-timed. She certainly had not intended to cause a scene and looked up to Jesus. His approving smile was all she needed to see.

What qualities do you admire in Mary?

Do you know someone who displays a similar purity of devotion to God?

Can you relate to the relationship between Mary and Jesus? If yes, how?

Can you understand how Jesus was central to Mary's life and focus? Describe how Jesus was everything to her.

Do you sense the soul intimacy between Mary and Jesus? She seemed to be confident in His love for her and was comfortable expressing her love for Him.

Why was Mary compelled to express her devotion to Jesus at this moment?

Jesus had previously affirmed His delight when Mary chose to sit at His feet and listen intently to every word He spoke. Mary undoubtedly felt comfortable in His presence and free to express herself. She followed an impulse of her heart, borne out of an overwhelming gratitude to the man, the Son of God, who had touched her life. She did not hesitate to convey her adoration, knowing that there might not be another time or place to express her feelings.

What caused her to do this? Explain how Mary's understanding of who Jesus was impacted her so profoundly that she would willingly give her precious possession and expose herself to public scrutiny.

If you were in attendance at this dinner, would you feel uncomfortable with Mary's display of adulation?

Would her actions seem "showy" or emotional to you?

Or might you have feelings of jealousy?

Mary was extravagant in her anointing and washing Jesus' feet — symbolic to say, "this is no ordinary guest and I am deeply devoted to Him." Though it was a servant's job to wash a guest's feet with *water*, Mary displayed humility by letting her hair down (which was unusual for a woman to do in public) and wiping His *perfumed* feet with her locks. Even in the presence of others who knew her, Mary was rebuked because of her outlandish actions. But Mary offered her *best* in sacrificial love while others, specifically Judas, could not see past the tangible worth of an object.

Has there been a time when you have been "scolded" for a passionate or sacrificial expression of your belief in Jesus? If so, describe the situation and explain your reaction.

Face-To-Face With Jesus

Jesus was fully aware of the dynamics of this scene. On the one hand, His friend Mary had intentionally poured her treasure on His head and feet and was now humbly bowing before Him out of the deepest expression of a heart filled with gratitude and worship. On the other hand, His disciples were criticizing her for what they judged to be an inappropriate and wasteful action. All they could see was the monetary cost of the perfume, though presenting their scolding as a concern for the poor. Their accusing hearts spoke volumes and the contrast did not go unnoticed.

Jesus saw kneeling before Him a woman after God's own heart — transparent, genuine, devoted, surrendered and pure as the oil of spikenard used to anoint Him. Unlike many of the other women He had encountered, Mary's actions were not based on *her* unfulfilled needs, but on an overflowing desire to give to *Him*.

What intensity of devotion does Jesus see when He looks into *your* heart? Describe your level of adoration of Jesus.

Does Jesus see a heart like Mary's, overwhelmed and bubbling over with gratitude and worship?

Are you aching to find a way to demonstrate your devotion to Him?

Do you long to see Jesus face-to-face and joyfully hope for an eternity in His presence?

I have asked one thing from the Lord; it is what I desire: to dwell in the house of the Lord all the days of my life, gazing on the beauty of the Lord and seeking [Him] in His temple. Psalm 27:4 HCSB

But I will see Your face in righteousness; when I awake, I will be satisfied with Your presence. Psalm 17:15 HCSB

Does your life revolve around seeking Jesus, expecting Him to show up, listening for His voice, yearning to spend every moment learning about His heart and preparing for a lifetime with Him?

Could it be said the expression of your love for Jesus, like Mary's, is passion-filled and sacrificial?

I will praise You with all my heart, Lord my God, and will honor Your name forever. Psalm 86:12 HCSB

Do you have a reputation of being unashamedly "sold out" for Jesus, with your life wholly dedicated to Him?

Do you willingly and sacrificially give of your time, possessions, talents and heart to God?

Would Jesus say that you are expressive of your love for Him?

I will declare your name to my people; in the assembly I will praise you. Psalm 22:22 NIV

I will praise the LORD at all times; His praise will always be on my lips. I will boast in the LORD; the humble will hear and be glad. Psalm 34:1-2 HCSB

Are there barriers to your enthusiastic declaration of love for Jesus? What causes your reticence?

Do you wish for heartfelt courage to demonstrate your affection to Jesus, but are embarrassed, afraid or hesitant to express your feelings about Jesus to others or in front of others? Why do you think this is?

Do you feel uncomfortable praising Jesus? Can you admit to what is holding you back from unrestrained praise? Are you ashamed in any way?

Are you struggling to worship and serve Jesus wholeheartedly?

Do you want to surrender your will to Him, but have difficulty completely "letting go" and worshipping with all your heart?

I will give you thanks in the great assembly; among the throngs I will praise you. Psalm 35:18 NIV

May God be praised! He has not turned away my prayer or turned His faithful love from me. Psalm 66:20 HCSB

Can you honestly "own" any of these statements?

I'm afraid to tell others about my belief in God.
I feel embarrassed to share my love for Jesus.
I don't talk about God with others because they will think I'm a religious nut.
I'm not an emotional person. Worship is just hyped up feelings.
I don't feel comfortable expressing my feelings, especially in front of others.
It is hard to trust Jesus when I haven't seen Him.
My family will make fun of me if they know I am trying to follow God.
God knows I love Him — that's what's important.

Come and listen, all who fear God, and I will tell what He has done for me. Psalm 66:16 HCSB

Let all who seek You rejoice and be glad in You; let those who love Your salvation continually say, "God is great"! Psalm 70:4 HCSB

Mary had a pure heart — free to love adoringly, generously and authentically. She was able to humbly kneel before Jesus with a settled heart, knowing she was forgiven, free of guilt and worries. Mary was genuinely at rest in His presence, and she was able to express the closeness of a relationship based on admiration and love. In an act of vulnerability, she publicly exposed her true heart, losing herself in the process of giving.

Worshiping the LORD is sacred; he will always be worshiped. Psalm 19:9 CEV

How often do you come to Jesus only to worship and praise Him, not asking Him for anything?

Do you come to Jesus as Mary did, without requests, not clamoring for His attention or to have your needs met — but only because He deserves and delights in Your adoration?

How refreshing would it have been for the Son of God to receive this expression of worshipful affection?

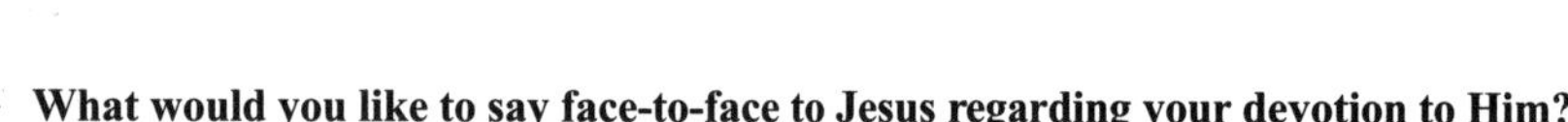

What would you like to say face-to-face to Jesus regarding your devotion to Him?

Words Spoken To The Heart

With perfume dripping from His head, He forcefully said to His disciples, "Leave her alone! Why are you bothering this woman?" Jesus stated that Mary had kept this perfume for the day of His burial and had done a beautiful thing for Him. Instead of condemning her, as the others had, Jesus commended her for this lovely act of kindness shown to Him before His anticipated death.

Jesus was not uncomfortable or embarrassed by this sincere display of devotion. He embraced her uninhibited expression of love. This was the second recorded time that a woman had poured oil over His feet and wiped them with her hair. What was perceived by the men in attendance as either scandalous or wasteful was affirmed by Jesus as an appropriate demonstration of worship and affection.

By defending Mary, Jesus implied that He too, placed a higher value on heartfelt worship than on physical possessions. Jesus did not disapprove of the use of physical possessions to help the poor, but expressed appreciation for the timing of Mary's adoration. Jesus reminded His disciples they would always have the poor with them, but *He* would not always be with them. Then He honored Mary by adding, "She did what she could do — in advance she poured perfume on My body to prepare it for My burial."

"She has done a beautiful thing for me." Matthew 26:10 CEV

How was Mary's adoration of Jesus "a beautiful thing"?

Do you sense how much Jesus delighted in Mary?

Describe how Mary's actions pleased Jesus.

Mary modeled what an intimate relationship with Jesus looks like. Essentially, hearts are connected. Jesus loves you! Therefore, You love Him and naturally express your devotion and adoration, even publicly, without consideration of cost. Jesus alone deserves your worship and your praise, and He delights in the expression of your devoted heart.

"Whoever acknowledges me before others, I will also acknowledge before my Father in heaven." Matthew 10:32 NIV

"And if anyone is not offended because of Me, he is blessed." Matthew 11:6 HCSB

In contrast:

"Anyone who does not honor the Son does not honor the Father who sent Him." John 5:23 HCSB

"For whoever is ashamed of Me and My words, the Son of Man will be ashamed of him when He comes in His glory and that of the Father and the holy angels." Luke 9:26 HCSB

How do you acknowledge and honor Jesus "before others"?

Are you able to joyfully declare, "I follow Jesus," "Jesus is my Lord," "Jesus is my Savior," and "I love Jesus!"?

Do you need to ask Jesus to free your heart so that you may genuinely and publicly express your love for Him?

"You can tell what a tree is like by the fruit it produces. You cannot pick figs or grapes from thornbushes. Good people do good things because of the good in their hearts. Bad people do bad things because of the evil in their hearts. Your words show what is in your heart." Luke 6:44-46 CEV

What do you passionately speak about from the overflow of your heart?

What dominates your conversation with others?

Is it apparent by your words and actions that you love Jesus?

Mary was privileged to worship Jesus face-to-face during His earthly presence. Our relationship is based on faith, and we worship in the Spirit and in truth. Even though we have not seen Him, we seek Him, worship Him, love Him and serve Him — faithfully knowing that He exists and loves us.

"Yet a time is coming and has now come when the true worshipers will worship the Father in the Spirit and in truth, for they are the kind of worshipers the Father seeks. God is spirit, and his worshipers must worship in the Spirit and in truth." John 4:23-24 NIV

Then Jesus told him, "Because you have seen me, you have believed; blessed are those who have not seen and yet have believed." John 20:29 NIV

"Love the Lord your God with all your heart and with all your soul and with all your mind and with all your strength." Mark 12:30 NIV

One of the chief expressions of love and service to Jesus is to love and serve others. How do you serve Jesus by serving others?

"Love your neighbor as yourself." Mark 29:31 NIV

"Whenever you did it for any of my people, no matter how unimportant they seemed, you did it for me." Matthew 25:40 CEV

"And anyone who gives one of my most humble followers a cup of cool water, just because that person is my follower, will surely be rewarded." Matthew 10:42 CEV

Have you ever sensed Jesus' appreciation for an act of devotion or a beautiful thing you have done for Him?

Do you realize that your relationship with Jesus could be similar to Mary of Bethany's — because He calls you His friend?

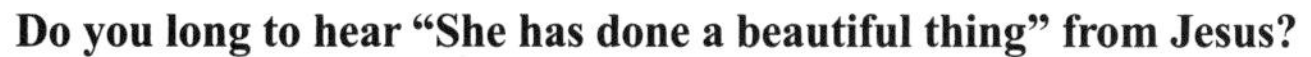

Do you long to hear "She has done a beautiful thing" from Jesus?

An Encounter With Jesus

Burial . . . Jesus had said it twice, confirming Mary's intuition of what was forthcoming! With the disciples quieted, she now was free to continue with wholehearted worship of her Lord, sharing intimacy with Jesus, knowing that any remaining time spent with Him was precious.

Mary placed her entire focus and identity in Jesus, unconcerned with the viewpoint of others or the cost of the perfume. Her relationship with Jesus demonstrated total belief in and dependence on Him. Mary gave Jesus her *all* — holding nothing back in communicating her reverence and devotion. And Mary gave Jesus her *best* — the best of her time, the best of her resources and the best of her heart. Every moment with Jesus counted. He was completely the focus of her being, and she loved Him with all her heart, soul, mind and strength.

Most important of all, because of Mary's extravagant expression of adoration, Jesus proclaimed that the story of the beautiful thing she did for Him during a dinner in the town of Bethany would be told throughout the world, in her memory.

How does Mary of Bethany inspire you?

Are you encouraged by her example to seek God relentlessly, passionately AND publicly?

How would you describe *your* relationship with Jesus?

Can you say without a doubt that *you* are Jesus' friend?

Do you give Jesus your best?

How would you like your relationship with Jesus to change or improve?

What would you like to say to Jesus?

Lord, please help me overcome any barriers that prevent my wholehearted worship of You. Purify my heart to reflect my gratitude for who You are and what You have done for me — how You have rescued me, redeemed me and called me to be Your friend. Tear down the chains that hold me back from sharing the story of Your life and boundless love. Help me to be free to demonstrate my devotion to You because of my overflowing heart.

Come, let us bow down in worship, let us kneel before the Lord our Maker. Psalm 95:6 NIV

For You are my hope, Lord GOD, my confidence from my youth. I have leaned on You from birth; You took me from my mother's womb. My praise is always about You. Psalm 71:5-6 HCSB

Do you have a growing desire to publicly speak words of devotion about your Jesus?

Are you compelled to tell others how much you love God?

From the day I was born, I have been in your care, and from the time of my birth, you have been my God. Psalm 22:10 CEV

Our Lord, I will sing of your love forever. Everyone yet to be born will hear me praise your faithfulness. I will tell them, "God's love can always be trusted, and his faithfulness lasts as long as the heavens." Psalm 89:1-2 CEV

How are you able to demonstrate your devotion to Jesus, as Mary did?

Do you serve Jesus because of His out-flowing love for you? Explain what this looks like.

How will you know that these acts of service flow from a loving heart toward Jesus?

I am eager to learn all that you want me to do; help me to understand more and more. Psalm 119:32 CEV

What does faith-driven devotion to Jesus look like?

What does it mean to "*love the Lord with all your heart*"?

What does a woman's life look like when she is a fully committed and devoted follower of Jesus?

Shout praises to the Lord! The Lord blesses everyone who worships him and gladly obeys his teachings. Psalm 112:1 CEV

You have shown me the path to life, and you make me glad by being near to me. Sitting at your right side, I will always be joyful. Psalm 16:11 CEV

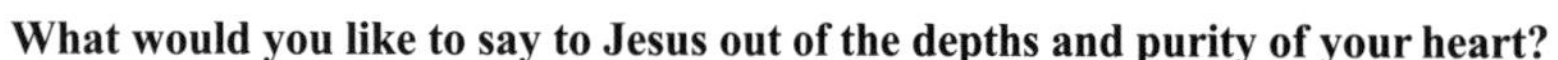

What would you like to say to Jesus out of the depths and purity of your heart?

Your Encounter With Jesus

Jesus, what do You want to teach me through Mary of Bethany's story? Write what you are hearing Him say to you.

Is Jesus saying, **"She has done a beautiful thing for me"**?

My Prayer For You

Sovereign God, Ruler of the universe, You alone are deserving of praise because of who You are, Your nature and Your power. May You open this woman's eyes and give her a glimpse of Your divine presence in her life so that she may hold You in highest esteem and adore You. May she grow to love You wholeheartedly and beautifully — with her entire heart, soul, mind, and body. Release her hesitancy, if any, to praise You by putting Your words of truth and a song in her heart. Plant words of worship on her lips and fill her with overflowing love such that her feet dance with joy in Your presence. Present opportunities for her to lavishly express devotion to You through adoration and service. Please increase her confidence so that she may boldly tell others of Your amazing love and of her relationship with You. I pray this in Jesus' beautiful name. Amen.

Your Prayer

Thoughts Regarding Your Journey Experience

One Final Act Of Kindness

John 19:25-27

No woman in the Bible is more honored than Mary, the mother and appointed guardian of the Son of God. Her song of praise for a God-given assignment is an example of sincere surrender to God's plan and a source of inspiration for us all. Though Mary reaped the joy and blessings of being Jesus' mother, she also sacrificed much. This mother's faith was strengthened as she trusted that her son's life, suffering and death were according to God's will.

Dear Woman, Here Is Your Son.

As a mother, Mary demonstrated faith by relinquishing control of her son's journey and destiny. She entrusted her Jesus into God's care, not seeing the complete picture of His seemingly tragic end. All humans are grateful to this dear woman for her dedication and service to her son and our Savior, Jesus.

In Her Shoes

"Mary, come quickly! They are going to crucify Jesus!" The ordeal had begun. She had already been awake throughout the night after reports of His arrest, and she was confident He would be found innocent of any wrongdoing and released. But crucified? There must be some mistake! Initially, Mary was frantic, but she silently prayed for peace. Her challenge had always been to navigate between being the human mother of Jesus and the mother of God's Son. It had been difficult to temper her maternal inclinations and emotional viewpoint with the knowledge that Jesus was also the Son of God who had a divine appointment and mission that she did not clearly understand.

Accompanied by her friends, she hurried through the streets while moving toward the rancorous noise that filled the air. The streets were lined with people shaking their fists and spitting at the three men trudging along the cobblestone pathway. Each man labored under the weight of a cross he was required to carry to the crucifixion site. How could this be? One of the men was her Jesus! A wave of nausea overcame Mary, and the women held her tightly when her knees buckled. She felt faint.

Mary could not even begin to grasp the level of hatred and cruelty that would bring humans to treat others like this. None of this made any sense to her, but there was no way to escape the horrific reality of the circumstances. Her son was about to die, through no fault of His own. No, no! They have it all wrong! Don't they know that this is God's very own Son — *her* son? The cursing and feverish shouting drowned out her cries as she watched Jesus stumble and fall. The soldiers grabbed a man from the crowd and forced him to carry Jesus' cross.

On they trudged, one grueling step after the other, until they reached Golgotha. Mary refused to watch as each of Jesus' hands was nailed to the cross beam. She covered her ears to block out the screams when the nails went through His feet and the cross was hoisted into an upright position.

Words cannot begin to describe the physical and emotional condition of Mary as she followed the crucifixion procession of Jesus through the streets of Jerusalem and to the foot of the cross that constrained Him. Though she was consumed with grief at watching her son suffer, the depth of her feelings was intensified because of the exceptional bond she had with this condemned man. From Jesus' conception by the Holy Spirit, their relationship was anything but normal. Although Mary was mother to additional children, Jesus was undeniably special.

Only a woman of internal strength and divine guidance could have dealt with her God-given assignment. As Jesus' mother, Mary's life had already been complicated. She courageously persevered during a scandalous virgin pregnancy.

After giving birth in a less than desirable stable, she made a hasty escape to Egypt, protecting her son from raging King Herod. These sacrifices she knowingly and willingly made, trusting God's promises that had been spoken to her by an angel.

Mary knew her son had a unique destiny because the angel told her to name her baby Jesus, meaning "The Lord saves." But nothing had prepared her for this final scene. Jesus' face was barely recognizable after the brutal beating and scourging He had received at the hands of the Romans. Sure, He was a grown man, but this was her firstborn son. Treasured memories of His special childhood came to her mind. What a joy Jesus had been! He brought so much life into their home with His curious and creative nature. She remembered the lessons at the kitchen table as Scriptures were learned and discussed. Even as a young boy, He paid special interest to those who were disadvantaged, defending the disabled against the cruel remarks of bullies. She would beam with pride when neighbors would comment on His kindness, compassion and wisdom.

Quiet moans brought her back to reality. This was her own dear son, nailed to a cross, doomed to die. How precious Jesus was to her.

Though they shared a close mother-to-son relationship, Mary knew she eventually had to share Jesus with the world and had mixed feelings about His growing independence. She had a flashback to a frantic three-day search for Jesus when He was twelve years old. They found Him in the temple courts sitting among the teachers engaged in discussion, confident of His decision to be "in His Father's house."

As He grew in height and strength from carpentry work with her husband Joseph, Jesus also seemed to become increasingly moved by the injustices and suffering He witnessed. The passion in His voice and fire in His eyes intrigued Mary as she waited for signs of His prophesied power. The bond of a mother would naturally be intense, but coupled with the divine circumstances of His conception and prophetic mission, Mary watched Him with admiration, maybe even with curiosity. So when the wine ran out during the wedding festivities they were attending in the village of Cana, she approached Jesus, anticipating a display of His miraculous power. She had an inkling of His destiny and believed in Him, telling the servants, "Do whatever He tells you!" His first public miracle of changing water into wine confirmed what she had held in her heart for years.

Mary had watched from a distance as Jesus fully engaged in ministry by healing the sick, restoring sight to the blind, teaching and providing food for the masses. She too, was awed by the miracles, but was the only person in the crowd who could say to herself, "That's my son!" Though Jesus' focus was always on His mission, He always seemed to be aware of her presence and there continued to be a special connection when their eyes met. It still was difficult to let go and allow Him to fulfill His prophetic role, whatever that was to mean. Mary understood His ministry of miracles as confirmation of His identity as the Son of God. But she had no hint of the intense suffering He would face — the public ridicule, eventual arrest, scourging and now this sentence of death via crucifixion.

It seemed so surreal, but there she stood watching this man die. While others loved Jesus because of the roles He played in their lives, such as Teacher and Healer, she saw this man through a mother's eyes. This man was her adored child. It also seemed so final. She could barely stand, as she was exhausted, numbed with shock and grief. Her sorrow was overwhelming. Maybe this is what Simeon meant when he spoke over her eight-day-old Jesus at the temple — "A sword will pierce your own soul, too."

She was confused. How could He be the Messiah, the Son of God, while nailed to a cross? Though she did not understand, Mary trusted God just as she had done when the angel appeared to her announcing that she would be the one to bring God's Son into the world. And she knew that whatever happened was according to God's plan — His will for Jesus and for her.

Every now and then, Mary would look up to Jesus and offer Him a weak smile. The end must be near. Is He really going to leave me? How can this be possible that I'm losing my son? I must stay strong for Him. Heavenly Father, she pleaded, this is more than I can bear.

Mary was grateful for her friends who were supporting her through this darkest day of her life. The empathetic disciple John reassured her with his gentle strength and comforting touch.

Jesus cleared His voice, as if attempting to speak, and Mary looked up into His face.

Which events in Mary's journey can you relate to?

Motherhood brings joys and heartaches. How do you relate to Mary's experience as a mother?

What aspects of being Jesus' mother would Mary have delighted in?

What was it about Mary's role of mother that it could be said of her son, "He grew in favor with God and man" (Luke 2:52)?

Does it help you relate to Mary's emotions at the foot of the cross because you are a mother?

Where do you imagine yourself to be in this scene? Would you be watching the agony of this man?

Would you have distanced yourself from this "rebel"? Would you be throwing curses toward Him? Or would you have followed Jesus through the streets of Jerusalem to the cross?

Face-To-Face With Jesus

Looking down from the cross at His mother, He understood the anguish she was enduring. This woman, the one who had carried Him in her womb after conception by the Holy Spirit and given Him birth, could barely look at Him because watching Him suffer was emotionally catastrophic.

But He also knew that just as her pain during childbirth was replaced by joy at the arrival of a son, in a matter of days her current sorrow would also turn to joy upon His appearance as the risen Christ. Of course, she could not see the outcome and was experiencing a mother's most terrifying agony — witnessing the suffering of her child, her Jesus.

Yes, Jesus understood the intense maternal bond that endured even when that child grew into manhood. He loved her so. She was His mother — the most significant woman in His life. She had devotedly been by His side from day one. Even after He publicly seemed to distance Himself from His family by claiming "whoever does God's will is My brother and sister and mother," she continued to love and follow Him.

Jesus also understood she would soon be alone and miss Him dearly. So, as He looked into His mother's heart, grieving at the impending loss of her son, He determined to honor her and make provision for her care.

Describe what Mary's heart could have been feeling during this traumatic time.

How was Mary's faith being tested?

What doubts could she have been struggling with?

What fears might Mary have been experiencing?

Mary was probably bewildered and confused, but continued to trust in God's will for Jesus' and her life. As with her entire journey as Jesus' mother, she courageously surrendered her doubts and fears and believed in and trusted God. Even though she could not see beyond the certainty of His death on the cross, Mary continued to hold on with her faithful heart that had been forged through many previous challenges and trials.

What does Jesus see when He looks into your heart as you kneel at His cross?

Do you have any of these thoughts?

I'm all alone.
I can't do this by myself.
It doesn't matter.
I don't matter.
I feel abandoned.
I don't understand what is happening.
God, how could You let this happen to me?
God is withholding good from me.
Can I trust God's heart for me?
I want to believe. Help me in my unbelief.
I can't count on anyone or I'll get let down.

What are your specific doubts regarding God?

What aspect of your life's journey has shaken your faith in God's goodness towards you?

My God, my God, why have You forsaken me? [Why are You] so far from my deliverance and from my words of groaning? My God, I cry by day, but You do not answer, by night, yet I have no rest. But You are holy, enthroned on the praises of Israel. Psalm 22:1-3 HCSB

I ask, "When will You comfort me? How many days [must] Your servant [wait]? Psalm 119:82, 84 HCSB

If you are a mother like Mary, what concerns or fears do you have regarding your children and their future?

Do you struggle to see God's hand in their lives?

Are you having a difficult time entrusting your children into God's capable hands?

I sought the LORD, and He answered me and delivered me from all my fears. Psalm 34:4 HCSB

Surely, LORD, you bless the righteous; you surround them with your favor as with a shield. Psalm 5:12 NIV

What would you like to ask Jesus to show you more clearly?

What areas in your life do you need to entrust to Jesus right now?

In what way do you need hope?

I lift up my eyes to the mountains — where does my help come from? My help comes from the LORD, the Maker of heaven and earth. Psalm 121:1-2 NIV

What would you like to say face-to-face to Jesus?

Words Spoken To The Heart

"Dear woman, this is your son." Though Jesus spoke with halted breath, the tone of gratitude and admiration for His mother was clear to those within earshot. The man by Mary's side, His close friend and disciple John, was now to stand in place of her son Jesus.

To His friend He said, "Here is your mother," indicating that from that point forward John would take the previously widowed Mary into His home and care for her — in Jesus' place.

Jesus knew John was uniquely gifted with the ability to love and that His mother would be well cared for while living in his household. John had supported Mary throughout this trying time and would be able to provide for her physical and emotional needs the rest of her days. John would also be able to offer the special love that only a son can give to his mother. Jesus entrusted John to ensure Mary's status and reputation would be upheld with dignity, knowing that public scrutiny associated with His trial and death would be intense.

So, Jesus' final act of compassion was reserved for His own dear mother — the one woman selected to bear, nurture and raise the Son of God. While taking on the sins of the entire world, Jesus still had the presence of mind to focus on one woman, His mother.

"Dear woman, here is your son." John 19:26 NIV

What thoughts and emotions surface when you hear Jesus call His mother *"dear woman"*?

What was the significance of His words *"here is your son"*?

Can you imagine how Mary felt when she heard her dying son, her grown child, speak those words to her? Would she have been comforted?

Why did Jesus add the phrase spoken to John, *"here is your mother"*?

Jesus' sacrificial act on the cross was for the entirety of humanity, yet was personal to each individual who has lived and to those who will be born in the future. As Jesus hung on the cross, dying as Savior for the entire world, He demonstrated His enduring love for His mother and her faithful heart. And just as He was aware of His dear mother and provided for her, He has the ability and power to seek you out and provide for your needs. His heart is for *you*! He died so that you can have life!

Do you believe that Jesus is Savior for the world and *your* personal Savior?

Do you truly believe that Jesus loves *you*, dear woman?

Though we know that after Jesus' death Mary saw Him again in resurrected form, can you empathize with her sense of loss as she witnessed His final breaths?

How would Jesus' words provide comfort, though Mary did not understand them completely?

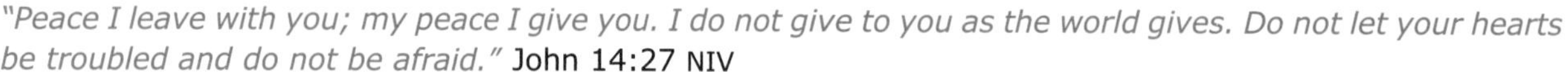

"Peace I leave with you; my peace I give you. I do not give to you as the world gives. Do not let your hearts be troubled and do not be afraid." John 14:27 NIV

Before leaving this world, Jesus reassured His followers, including His mother, that they would see Him again. Though they could not see the details clearly, their only hope was to faithfully trust that His words were true.

"So with you: Now is your time of grief, but I will see you again and you will rejoice, and no one will take away your joy." John 16:22 NIV

"Your heart must not be troubled. Believe in God; believe also in Me. In My Father's house are many dwelling places; if not, I would have told you. I am going away to prepare a place for you. If I go away and prepare a place for you, I will come back and receive you to Myself, so that where I am you may be also." John 14:1-3 HCSB

"You heard me say, 'I am going away and I am coming back to you.' If you loved me, you would be glad that I am going to the Father, for the Father is greater than I." John 14:28 NIV

Jesus also told His followers that He must go away so the Holy Spirit could come. He would not abandon or leave His followers alone. Therefore, He would send the Holy Spirit to live in and assist His believers on their journey as they awaited their reunion in heaven.

"But I tell you that I am going to do what is best for you. That is why I am going away. The Holy Spirit cannot come to help you until I leave. But after I am gone, I will send the Spirit to you." John 16:7 CEV

"I tell you the truth, if you have faith as small as a mustard seed, you can say to this mountain, 'Move from here to there' and it will move. Nothing will be impossible for you." Matthew 17:20 NIV

Can you imagine how Mary cherished the Holy Spirit after Jesus was no longer with her?

Are you convinced that you are eternally safe because of Jesus' love and provision for *you*?

"My sheep hear My voice, I know them, and they follow Me. I give them eternal life, and they will never perish — ever! No one will snatch them out of My hand. My Father, who has given them to Me, is greater than all. No one is able to snatch them out of the Father's hand. The Father and I are one." John 10:27-30 HCSB

"Father, I don't ask you to take my followers out of the world, but keep them safe from the evil one." John 17:15 CEV

Do you believe that Jesus is coming again? What is the significance of His second coming?

Just as Jesus came to this physical earth and lived with men and women, He has given us the opportunity to live with Him forever! Can you imagine how Mary longed for the future time when she would be with her dear son again — for all eternity!?

"Look! I am coming quickly, and My reward is with Me to repay each person according to what he has done. I am the Alpha and the Omega, the First and the Last, the Beginning and the End." Revelation 22:12-13 HCSB

Then I saw a new heaven and a new earth, for the first heaven and the first earth had passed away, and the sea existed no longer. I also saw the Holy City, new Jerusalem, coming down out of heaven from God, prepared like a bride adorned for her husband. Then I heard a loud voice from the throne: Look! God's dwelling is with men, and He will live with them. They will be His people, and God Himself will be with them and be their God. He will wipe away every tear from their eyes. Death will exist no longer; grief, crying, and pain will exist no longer, because the previous things have passed away. Revelation 21:1-6 HCSB

Summarize your thoughts about Mary's son, Jesus. What impact has His life and death had on you?

What does it mean to know that Jesus was Immanuel, "God with us" (Matthew 1:23) — and that He came to save *you*?

Do you believe that Jesus died for the sins of the entire world, including *your* sins? He took upon Himself the consequence for human sin — death — willingly placing Himself on the cross and dying for every human born.

"And I, when I am lifted up from the earth, will draw all people to myself." John 12:32 NIV

What would you like to say to Mary's Jesus, *your* Jesus, regarding His sacrifice on the cross?

Would you like to ask Him to help you understand more deeply the significance of His life and death?

Are you clear as to your standing in God's eyes and how Jesus reconciled you to His heavenly Father?

At the beginning of time, humans were created in the image and likeness of God (Genesis 1:26) and intended to live in relationship with Him. With one act of disobedience, the original humans rebelled against God, radically altering their spiritual relationship. God, in the Person of Jesus, God's Son, was miraculously born of a virgin woman and willingly dwelled with us. He took upon Himself the rebellion and sin of humanity in order to restore the relationship between humans and God, making it possible for all to live eternally in God's presence. Because of Jesus' sacrificial death on the cross, we are now reconciled to God and stand blameless in His presence.

How has your understanding of grace deepened while walking in Mary's shoes?

Jesus, the Son of God, was born of this faithful woman, lived as a man and died as your Savior to give you eternal life — because of grace. Not because of your own strength or goodness — but by His loving gift of grace.

"For God loved the world in this way: He gave His One and Only Son, so that everyone who believes in Him will not perish but have eternal life." John 3:16 HCSB

"Just as the Son of Man did not come to be served, but to serve, and to give His life — a ransom for many." Matthew 20:28 HCSB

Jesus' gift of reconciliation to God is given to us by grace. It is each person's choice to acknowledge that Jesus is the Savior of the world and accept this gift of eternal life.

Will you choose, or have you chosen, to believe that God has chosen, forgiven and reconciled *you* to Him through Jesus?

Will you accept His grace and sacrifice for your sins and proclaim Jesus as your Savior and Lord?

Have you embraced the truth of reconciliation? How have you experienced reconciliation with God?

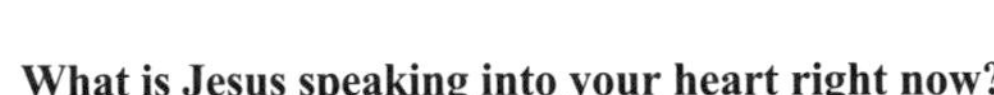

What is Jesus speaking into your heart right now?

An Encounter With Jesus

Even though He was in excruciating agony, Jesus was concerned for the hearts of others, specifically His mother's, with her cries of grief. He looked down on this blessed woman, His mother Mary, and honored her by ensuring she would be safe, provided for and treated with loving kindness because of her significant role in His life.

Soon after His comforting words, Jesus let out a loud cry and breathed His last breath. It was finished! A terrifying earthquake punctuated the pivotal moment in history. After a soldier jabbed a spear in His side, Mary remained to watch His lifeless body taken down from the cross. She followed as He was laid in a tomb. A large stone was rolled over the entrance and those gathered paused to grasp the finality of the moment. After lingering by His grave, Mary went home with John, drained and empty. Only time would be able to resolve her seemingly hopeless situation.

She DID see her Jesus again, this time as the resurrected Son of God, the world's Savior! Oh, the joy of their reunion! All was well! However, Mary would continue to miss His presence — seeing His smiling face, hearing His voice, feeling His embrace — after He ascended to heaven (Acts 1:9). The big picture was now clear, and she felt extremely blessed to have been Jesus' mother.

Jesus understands the heart of a mother when she has to witness her child suffering. He hears the cries of a mother's heart when a child is ill, hurting or in distress. He also understands that the trials in our present reality are nothing to be compared with the promise of a glorious eternity with Him. Yes, Jesus understands and He is kind.

How does the example of Jesus' mother inspire or encourage you?

Do you feel that you have been chosen for a mission of significance? Explain.

Do you see how you are part of a larger story? Do you believe Jesus has a plan for your life? Write an overview of your journey with God.

Where do you not see the details? What are your challenges?

When the angel Gabriel appeared to Mary and told her that she would give birth to God's Son and name Him Jesus, she had her doubts.

"How can this be, since I am a virgin?" The angel replied to her: "The Holy Spirit will come upon you, and the power of the Most High will overshadow you. Therefore the holy One to be born will be called the Son of God . . . For nothing will be impossible with God." Luke 1:34-35, 37 NIV, HCSB

Does Mary's journey encourage you to faithfully walk with Jesus, no matter the cost or where He takes you?

Do you trust His goodness toward you?

Do you trust in His plan for your life? Can you surrender your self-direction into His capable hands?

Do you believe God's promises to you?

Which words of Jesus do you treasure in your heart?

Though Mary had her doubts, her response is testimony to her faith in God's plan for her life.

Mary said, "I am the Lord's servant! Let it happen as you have said." Luke 1:38 CEV

Do you have a willing and obedient heart like Jesus' mother?

Do you have faith that whatever God asks you to do for Him, He will equip you for the task and guide you through the journey?

Without seeing the outcome or understanding what would be required of her, Mary praised God:

"My soul glorifies the Lord and my spirit rejoices in God my Savior, for he has been mindful of the humble state of his servant. From now on all generations will call me blessed, for the Mighty One has done great things for me — holy is his name." Luke 1:46-49 NIV

Even though you do not see the outcome of God's will for *your* life, can you praise Him?

What doubts, fears, worries or anxieties does God want you to surrender to His control and timing?

What will you do when your relationship with Jesus seems distant or quiet? Will you continue to trust Him?

How will you respond when your life seems opposed or contrary to your expectations?

Have you determined to diligently seek Jesus and His direction for your life, regardless of your circumstances?

How does Mary's faithful example encourage you to surrender your life completely to God's will for you?

Mary's unique story emphasizes the valuable role that a mother plays in her child's life. Every child is a gift from God and created for His delight and glory. When a mother is entrusted with one of God's children, she has the opportunity to model Jesus' love for the child. And when a woman is a willing partner with God while raising a child, she has a profound impact on that child's physical and eternal life.

Mothers, do you see your role as a significant mission?

In what ways do you look to Mary as a role model of mothering?

Do you delight in your season of mothering in the same way that Mary delighted in mothering Jesus? Explain.

What do you think was Mary's greatest gift to her son Jesus?

How strongly do you feel the greatest gift you can give your child is the perspective of eternity — that God loves your child and longs to spend eternity in an intimate relationship with him or her?

Are there aspects of your mothering role that can be refocused to ensure that your children "grow in favor with God and man," like Jesus did?

Mothers, in what ways to do you need to release your children to God's care, trusting that He will carry them through their journey?

What specific requests do you bring to Jesus on behalf of your child/children?

What specific requests do you bring to Jesus regarding your role of mothering?

Because you are my help, I sing in the shadow of your wings. My soul clings to you; your right hand upholds me. Psalm 63:7-8 NIV

Mary's encounter with Jesus was truly unique. When Jesus was a child, Mary provided love and safety for Him. Now, as a grown man, He lovingly and tenderly provided for *her* care. Jesus' interaction with this "dear woman," his mother, gives a glimpse into the love Jesus has for *you*. Through the Holy Spirit, Jesus still comforts, provides for, protects, rescues and cherishes.

You are my hiding place! You protect me from trouble, and you put songs in my heart because you have saved me. You said to me, "I will point out the road that you should follow. I will be your teacher and watch over you." Psalm 32:7-8 CEV

The one who lives under the protection of the Most High dwells in the shadow of the Almighty. Psalm 91:1 HCSB

The Lord says, "If you love me and truly know who I am, I will rescue you and keep you safe. When you are in trouble, call out to me. I will answer and be there to protect and honor you. You will live a long life and see my saving power." Psalm 91:14-16 CEV

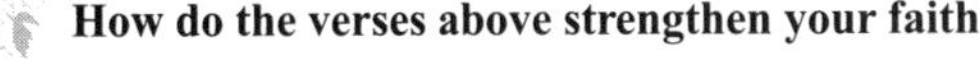

How do the verses above strengthen your faith?

Just as Mary trusted that she would see Jesus again (as He had told her), we wait and hope for the time when He will return (as He has told us).

We wait for the Lord; He is our help and shield. For our hearts rejoice in Him, because we trust in His holy name. May Your faithful love rest on us, Lord, for we put our hope in You. Psalm 33:20-22 HCSB

You are my place of safety and my shield. Your word is my only hope. Psalm 119:114 CEV

How are you using the time God has given you on earth (while you wait)?

In what ways do you sense Jesus is asking you to serve Him (while you wait)? Do you consistently ask Him for guidance?

Are there "little ones" Jesus has entrusted into your care (while you wait)?

Is Jesus calling you to an earthly mission as you anticipate eternity with Him?

What plan does He have for you now, in context of an eternal perspective?

What would you like to say to Jesus, Your Savior, right now?

Your Encounter With Jesus

Jesus, what do You want me to learn from Your mother's life of faith? Write what you are hearing Him say to you.

How is Jesus calling *you*, **"dear woman"**?

My Prayer For You

Lord, please call this "dear woman" by name and bless her by revealing Yourself more fully. Help her to surrender to Your perfect plan for her life. Strengthen her faith by relieving her doubts and by providing an eternal perspective for her life. If this "dear woman" is a mother, encourage her as she serves You by caring for Your precious little ones that You have blessed her with. Help her to release their lives into Your loving hands, as she guides them with Your words of truth. Holy Spirit, touch this woman so that she feels safe and secure in Your love. Comfort her now and give her bright hope of eternity with You. And as she waits to stand before you face-to-face, clearly show her Your significant plan for her life and what You have purposed her to do on Your behalf. Jesus, our precious Savior, thank You for making this possible with Your life, death and resurrection. Jesus, I pray this in Your revered name. Amen!

Your Prayer

Thoughts Regarding Your Journey Experience

ENCOUNTER WITH THE RISEN JESUS

Mark 15:47, 16:9-11, Luke 23:55-56, 24:1-11, John 20:1-2, 11-18

Mary Magdalene was one of Jesus' most devoted followers. Remarkably, Jesus chose her, a woman with a less than glowing reputation, to announce that He had been resurrected and truly was alive! What made their relationship unique? Maybe it had something to do with the fact that Jesus delivered her from a life of mental torment and oppression so that she could live life to the full. Mary Magdalene demonstrated how a "chosen and freed" person expresses gratitude by loyally following Jesus through the darkest part of His mission, refusing to leave His presence, even in death.

Who Is It You Are Looking For?

IN HER SHOES

Mary Magdalene sat outside Jesus' tomb weeping with despair. It was not supposed to have happened this way, or so she thought. Jesus had told His followers He would be going away, but this was not how she had imagined it.

Jesus was her Teacher and Master, and she had given Him everything — her livelihood and her heart. Along with other women, Mary Magdalene followed him from town to town, supporting His traveling group with money and supplies. So totally committed to serving Him, she was not even concerned about her reputation. Many would try to paint her as an immoral woman with a romantic interest in Jesus. Yes, she knew people gossiped about her, but she also knew the truth. Oh, He was so much more than a man! Jesus was her Lord, the Son of God and the Messiah, chosen to save and redeem His people. Her reverence and awe of Jesus laid the foundation for the spiritual intimacy with Him that few understood or shared.

Something had drawn Mary to Jesus. It was His message that initially convicted her heart — a message of forgiveness, justice, redemption and hope. His message was in stark contrast to the abuse she had suffered in her life. Whereas people had treated her with contempt, Jesus spoke with respect and kindness.

Her belief in Him was strengthened as she witnessed miracles such as restoring sight to the blind and healing long standing infirmities and deformities. Mary had, in fact, been the recipient of a healing miracle herself, as Jesus released her from the suffering of being possessed by seven demons. No longer was she tormented by evil spirits and considered an outcast. Few understood the bondage of demon possession, the mental anguish and self-destructive behavior. But Jesus had graciously redeemed her from a bottomless pit and made her whole. Yes, she followed this man out of gratitude for the mercy He had extended to her. He had set her free and restored her life.

Mary's devotion to Jesus was not only due to the healing she received from Him. She came to believe in him as Truth — by listening to His parables and confrontations with Pharisees and by observing His example of compassion, mercy and forgiveness.

Mary loved being in His presence and faithfully stayed by the side of this condemned man named Jesus, who was scorned, beaten and crucified. Waves of grief had overwhelmed her as she watched His brutal and ignominious death on a cross. Joseph of Arimethea had provided a grave for Jesus' lifeless body. She watched as men lifted His corpse into the tomb and rolled a massive stone across the doorway. Mary returned to her home after His hasty burial, completely emotionally spent.

When the Sabbath was over, Mary Magdalene and other women headed for the tomb outside the city walls. They walked in a dazed motion, drained from the emotional upheaval of the past week's events, and brought sweet spices to complete the anointing process. As Mary entered the garden, she saw signs of the soldiers' post, including a smoldering fire and scattered equipment. But why had the stone been removed from the entrance? Weren't the guards posted there to keep watch over the sealed tomb?

Looking inside the tomb, she saw nothing, just the strips of linen that had bound her Lord. Not only had Mary's hopes been shattered with the death and burial of her beloved Jesus, but now His body was gone. Grave robbers! Frantically, she ran to tell Peter someone had taken the Lord's body.

Peter and others raced to the gravesite to see firsthand if what Mary said was true. After confirmation of her story, they left, leaving her alone with her bewildered thoughts. So there she sat, sobbing inconsolably. Her loss was devastating. "Will I ever see Jesus again? I miss Him so."

Not knowing where to turn, Mary decided it was time to go back home. She stood up and took one last look into the tomb. Two angels were now sitting on the cold slab where Jesus had been placed. "Woman, why are you crying?" they asked. Dejected and seemingly unfazed by their presence, Mary told them, "They took my Lord and I don't know where they have put Him."

Mary turned around and saw a man standing there. She was unaware it was Jesus.

Have you experienced Jesus in a similar way to Mary Magdalene? Explain how you relate to her story.

Have you lived with cruel mental chains similar to Mary's demons? Describe the debilitating effect on your life.

How would freedom from that oppression have changed Mary's life?

Have you experienced freedom from bondage in any way? What specific oppression were you released from?

Do you think that Jesus delighted in restoring Mary's life?

Does Mary's story give you hope by believing Jesus desires your redemption, restoration and freedom to live with eternal purpose?

Do you think redemption from demon possession was the primary reason Mary gratefully followed Jesus? Might there be other reasons?

What would it be like to be as relationally close to Jesus as Mary Magdalene? Describe.

How is a relationship with Jesus different than worldly love?

What does "unconditional" love imply? Does Jesus really love you without expecting anything in return?

Can you imagine what it would have been like to be Jesus' friend and travel with Him from town to town?

What would it look like for Mary Magdalene to be a friend of Jesus in today's world? How would we know that she is a friend and devoted follower of Jesus?

Face-To-Face With Jesus

Jesus looked through the eyes and into the heart of one of His courageous followers whom He knew so well. Mary Magdalene was special in many ways — grateful, faithful, committed and wholehearted. She had endured much ridicule in her life, first from being demon possessed and also when accompanying Him as He traveled from town to town. He had heard the wagging tongues and accusations hurled at her. Though it was considered scandalous for a woman to be in the company of men, He knew the purity of her devotion to Him. He also understood the depth of her loss. Her heart was breaking because of her love for *Him*.

Why was Mary searching for Jesus? Can you describe what she was feeling in her heart?

How was she lost without Him? Was she unconvinced He was truly gone?

Can you relate to her seemingly inconsolable longing for Jesus?

Do you think Mary was struggling with a sense of futility?

Do any of these statements sound familiar?

Is this all there is?
It's just not worth it.
I feel so alone.
I'm not sure I can go on.
Why don't I hear His voice?
Why do I feel distance in my relationship with Jesus?
I don't believe God loves me.

When I awake, all I want is to see you as you are. Psalm 17:15 CEV

Do you long to understand how a woman like Mary Magdalene could become so devoted to Jesus?

Does it seem like something is missing in your relationship with Him?

What might it take to compel you to follow Jesus with similar passion as Mary Magdalene?

Does that seem impossible under your circumstances?

Are there times when Jesus seems particularly quiet and it seems you are not hearing His voice clearly, or at all?

Though you know God loves you, do you still miss His tangible presence and wish to see Him face-to-face?

My heart says of you, "Seek his face!" Your face, Lord, I will seek. Psalm 27:8 NIV

Why do you think Jesus chose to appear first to Mary Magdalene?

What did Jesus love about Mary's heart? Did He see a heart purely devoted only to Him?

What does Jesus see when He looks into *your* heart?

How desperately do you desire to know Jesus better? Does your heart ache to see Him and to know Him more intimately?

Are you actively searching for Him? How does that "searching" manifest itself in your life?

Those who know Your name trust in You because You have not abandoned those who seek You, Lord. Psalm 9:10 HCSB

How or when do you miss the presence of Jesus in your life?

Have you ever said to Jesus, "I need You," "I miss You," "I can't wait to see You," "I'm desperate for You!"?

Do you sense His response? How has He responded?

Are you passionately consumed with pursuing His presence in your life? Does this include consistently reading Biblical words of truth?

Are you willing to seek Jesus relentlessly and wait for Him to "show up"?

Be silent before the Lord and wait expectantly for Him. Psalm 37:7 HCSB

Do you desire to know Him better, but not know how?

Could you be looking for Jesus by relying on someone else's relationship with Him? Do you seek *their* words of wisdom, prayers and guidance — but avoid intimate interaction with Him yourself?

If so, can you identify why? Does it seem too difficult or take too much time and effort to follow Jesus?

Do you think He would give you the strength and courage to pursue Him if you asked?

Search for the Lord and for His strength; seek His face always. Psalm 105:4 HCSB

What would you say to Jesus if you were standing face-to-face with Him?

Words Spoken To The Heart

"Woman, why are you crying? Who is it you are looking for?" Mary was still dazed by the events of the past three days and thinking He was the gardener, asked Him to tell her where the body was so that she could go get it herself.

"Mary!" She snapped out of her stupor when her name was called and looked intently at the face of this man. "Mary!" He had spoken her name! His voice sounded familiar. Could it be? This man spoke with the same warmth and loving tone that she had come to know while conversing with Jesus on their travels. Yes, she recognized that voice! It was Jesus — "Teacher!"

The change in her countenance was dramatic as she burst into a radiant smile. She could not contain her joy and rushed to cling to Him, a natural response of adoration and an indication of their comfortable relationship. Gently, He said, "Don't hold on to Me for I have not returned to My Father." Then He commissioned her to tell His followers of His resurrection and that He was going back to "My Father and your Father, to My God and your God."

"Who is it you are looking for?" John 20:15 NIV

Why do you think Jesus asked Mary that question?

How is Jesus' question significant to *you*?

***"Mary!"* Jesus knew her personally and called her by name! How did hearing her name impact Mary?**

Jesus knows *you* and is calling *you* by name! How does that statement impact you intellectually and emotionally?

Describe how it feels to realize that the Creator of the universe and Savior of the world knows *you* personally?

Maybe you have grown up with the notion that knowing about God through studying Scripture, attending church, performing religious rituals and observing denominational traditions is the way to salvation. Have you seen that the way to eternal life is through a *relationship* with Jesus?

"You pore over the Scriptures because you think you have eternal life in them, yet they testify about Me. And you are not willing to come to Me that you may have life." John 5:39-40 HCSB

"The Son of Man came to look for and to save people who are lost." Luke 19:10 CEV

Can you honesty admit that you need God? Have you humbly admitted that to Jesus?

Is it time to stop pretending that you are self-sufficient and do not need Jesus in your life?

What is keeping you from depending on God?

What will it take for you to confess that you cannot do "life" on your own human strength and that you need God — to be changed and given a new life?

"I am the vine, and you are the branches. If you stay joined to me, and I stay joined to you, then you will produce lots of fruit. But you cannot do anything without me." John 15:5 CEV

"Humans give life to their children. Yet only God's Spirit can change you into a child of God. Don't be surprised when I say that you must be born from above. Only God's Spirit gives new life." John 3:6-8 CEV

Have you journeyed through this workbook and still have doubts and questions about Jesus? Can you identify the core issue of your hesitance to believe in Jesus as your Savior?

What if it *is* true — that Jesus IS the prophesied Messiah? What will you be missing out on if you continue to resist the truth of God's love for you?

What do you have to lose if you choose to acknowledge Jesus as Savior?

What better options are there for you now and eternally, than belief in Jesus — the Messiah?

"Stop doubting and believe." John 20:27 NIV

Can you honestly admit your need for God's presence in your life?

Like Mary Magdalene, we all long to be known and loved unconditionally for who we are. This is our ultimate need. Are you convicted to believe in the unconditional love of Jesus, your Savior?

Have you accepted Jesus' invitation to life? If not, is this the time to believe in His grace and turn to Him as Lord of your life?

"All those the Father gives me will come to me, and whoever comes to me I will never drive away." John 6:37 NIV

"No one can come to me, unless the Father who sent me makes them want to come. But if they do come, I will raise them to life on the last day." John 6:44 CEV

"Listen! I am standing and knocking at your door. If you hear my voice and open the door, I will come in and we will eat together." Revelation 3:20 CEV

When Jesus called Mary's name, she saw her Healer, Redeemer, Master, Friend and Savior. Do you see Jesus as Mary did — not a taskmaster, or a genie to grant every wish, but as a most intimate friend?

Are you enjoying an intimacy with Jesus? What does this look like for you?

Jesus — "God with us" — experienced all aspects of humanity — hunger, pain, disappointment, betrayal, loss, loneliness, rejection, false accusation and death. How does it speak to your heart to know that only He knows exactly how you feel and all the details of your journey?

Do you have any remaining doubts as to Jesus' love for you?

"Greater love has no one than this: to lay down one's life for one's friends." John 15:13 NIV

For whom did Jesus lay down His life?

How has Jesus redeemed *you*?

How has Jesus saved *you*? Saved you from what?

How has Jesus taught and guided *you*?

In what other ways have you experienced Jesus?

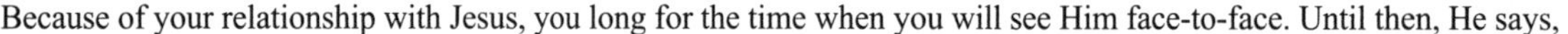

Because of your relationship with Jesus, you long for the time when you will see Him face-to-face. Until then, He says,

"I will be with you always, even until the end of the world." Matthew 28:20 CEV

How is this possible that He will always be *with* you — even *in* you?

"And I will ask the Father, and He will give you another Counselor to be with you forever. He is the Spirit of truth. The world is unable to receive Him because it doesn't see Him or know Him. But you do know Him, because He remains with you and will be in you." John 14:16-17 HCSB

"But the Counselor, the Holy Spirit, whom the Father will send in my name, will teach you all things and will remind you of everything I have said to you." John 14:26 NIV

"I will send you the Spirit who comes from the Father and shows what is true. The Spirit will help you and will tell you about me. Then you will also tell others about me, because you have been with me from the beginning." John 15:26-27 CEV

"When the Spirit of truth comes, He will guide you into all the truth." John 16:13 HCSB

How have you experienced the Holy Spirit in your life?

Jesus also has given us His words of truth. These words will set us free from the lies of the deceiver, Satan (John 8:44). How important is it for you to consistently seek truth?

How does truth bring joy into your life?

"Your word is the truth. So let this truth make them completely yours." John 17:17 CEV

"I have given myself completely for their sake, so that they may belong completely to the truth." John 17:19 CEV

"I have spoken these things to you so that My joy may be in you and your joy may be complete." John 15:11 HCSB

Is Jesus calling you and asking, "Who is it you are looking for?" What would you like to say to Him?

An Encounter With Jesus

What a profound encounter this was! It gave Jesus great joy to reveal Himself as the resurrected Christ first to a woman dogged by a negative reputation. All the more striking, as this was during a time when women could not be used as witnesses in legal proceedings, Jesus entrusted a *woman* with His message. So, of all His followers, Mary Magdalene was blessed to be the first person to say the words, "I have seen the Lord!"

No longer distraught, Mary was elated and raced to tell His disciples the good news. Initially they did not believe her, but soon they would also see their risen Lord, speak with Him and touch Him. No other event in the history of mankind has had such a significant outcome. Mary's jubilant proclamation, "I have seen the Lord!" changed everything and set world events on a new course.

Oh, there would be false witnesses bribed to claim that this historic event was staged and the body was stolen by His disciples. But Mary would testify otherwise. She, along with numerous others would risk their lives as witnesses to the truth of this good news — that Jesus once confirmed dead, was now confirmed alive!

For Mary Magdalene, this good news, this *great* news, revolved around a fairly simple story of who this man Jesus was. He was the Son of God born as prophesied of a virgin, Mary, whom she personally knew. His ministry proclaimed love, forgiveness, redemption, healing and hope for all humanity.

Jesus demonstrated that He, as God's Son, had power over death, bringing back to life a widow's dead son and His friend Lazarus. And just as He foretold, that same power raised Him from *His* grave. Jesus' resurrection power confirmed the truth of all aspects of His message and ministry. Jesus was no mere mortal, and He had the authority and power to heal, forgive, and save.

It all became clear to Mary. The improbable, impossible and unthinkable had truly taken place! Prophecies had been fulfilled. Jesus was Immanuel, God with us (Matthew 1:23). The Messiah had come, had died, had been raised after three days and three nights and now was with His heavenly Father. Yes, it was a true, compelling and simple story to tell. She was an eyewitness to His *humanity* and to His *divinity*, and she could not suppress her joy in the complete revelation of this truth. She personally had known this man and was witness to the fact that He overcame the grave, conquering death. Jesus was all He said He was — God's Son, the Truth, Bread of Life, The Way, the Resurrection and Life, Light of the World, True Vine, a King — the great I AM.

Mary also had a testimony of her personal encounter with Jesus. Her story, though indescribably amazing, was equally simple and easy to share. She, a sinner, broken and outcast, was reclaimed by Jesus' mercy, grace and unconditional love. As an individual, Mary Magdalene had experienced the totality of who Jesus was and is. Just as Psalm 103:3-5 claimed, she was the recipient of Jesus' benefits and was forgiven, healed, redeemed, valued and loved. She was blessed with an intimate relationship with Jesus that was different from a worldly love. Jesus loved her without any expectations and His was a sacrificial love.

Jesus appeared to His followers over a period of forty days and spoke about the Kingdom of God (Acts 1:3). Their gatherings were joyful occasions filled with praise and thanksgiving for this most extraordinary event — the resurrection of Jesus. Most likely, Mary Magdalene was there when His believers met together (Acts 1:14) while waiting expectantly to be baptized with the Holy Spirit (Acts 1:5, 8).

Life for Mary Magdalene changed the moment she encountered Jesus. She was blessed to be a personal eyewitness to His life, death and resurrection, and she lived out her remaining days full of the Holy Spirit and empowered to boldly share the message of hope for life in eternity with her Lord and Savior, her friend Jesus.

Dear woman, who is it *you* are looking for?

Are you searching for Someone and have restless or unfulfilled areas of your heart?

The Person you are looking for is Jesus! Open your eyes; He may be standing right in front of you, but you don't recognize Him. Listen for Him to call your name, to beckon you with an unmistakable invitation. Have you heard Jesus say, *"Come to Me"*?

Jesus is alive — raised from the grave that could not contain Him! Mary Magdalene was witness to that! The testimony of those who saw Him after His bodily resurrection confirmed prophecy and His words.

He said to them, "Why are you troubled, and why do doubts rise in your minds? Look at my hands and my feet. It is I myself! Touch me and see; a ghost does not have flesh and bones, as you see I have." Luke 24:38-39 NIV

Why do you think Jesus commissioned Mary Magdalene to tell His disciples that He had risen from His tomb?

How did Mary's journey with Jesus prepare her to be trusted with His message?

The LORD confides in those who fear him. Psalm 25:14 NIV

When Mary Magdalene first encountered Jesus, she believed in Him and became one of His followers in response to the miraculous and saving acts He performed in her life. After she encountered the resurrected Jesus, she began to tell the world the story of the Messiah. Mary and other believers risked their lives as they confidently spoke as witnesses to the events of His life, words, ministry, death, resurrection and ascension.

He told them: The Scriptures say that the Messiah must suffer, then three days later he will rise from death. They also say that all people of every nation must be told in my name to turn to God, in order to be forgiven. So beginning in Jerusalem, you must tell everything that has happened. I will send you the one my Father has promised, but you must stay in the city until you are given power from heaven. Luke 24:46-49 CEV

"Come, follow me, Jesus said, "and I will send you out to fish for people." Matthew 4:19 NIV

"You did not choose Me, but I chose you. I appointed you that you should go out and produce fruit and that your fruit should remain, so that whatever you ask the Father in My name, He will give you." John 15:16 HCSB

Who did Mary tell about her friend and Savior, Jesus?

Why do you think it was so important for her to tell others?

Are you as convinced about Jesus as Mary Magdalene was?

Who do *you* want to tell about Jesus?

What will you say? What story will you share with others?

Then Jesus came to them and said, "All authority in heaven and on earth has been given to me. Therefore go and make disciples of all nations, baptizing them in the name of the Father and of the Son and of the Holy Spirit, and teaching them to obey everything I have commanded you. And surely I am with you always, to the very end of the age." Matthew 28:18-20 NIV

Does the commission from Jesus to "go, baptize and teach" apply to you? In what ways?

Have you accepted the same mission Jesus gave to His followers as a personal calling? Or is that only for religious leaders?

Have you yourself been baptized in the name of the Father, the Son and the Holy Spirit?

Can you passionately and genuinely say to someone, "Come and see my Jesus!"?

Can you confidently say, "God rescued me through the life, death and resurrection of His Son, Jesus, and called me to be reconciled to God, to come to an eternal home through faith in Christ, the Messiah"?

How can I repay the LORD all the good He has done for me? Psalm 116:12 HCSB

Only goodness and faithful love will pursue me all the days of my life, and I will dwell in the house of the LORD as long as I live. Psalm 23:6 HCSB

Shortly after Jesus was resurrected, He appeared to His disciples and said to them:

"Peace to you! As the Father has sent Me, I also send you." After saying this, He breathed on them and said, "Receive the Holy Spirit." John 20:21-22 HCSB

Have you received the Holy Spirit?

How has the gift of the Holy Spirit impacted your life?

While He was together with them, He commanded them not to leave Jerusalem, but to wait for the Father's promise. "This," [He said, "is what] you heard from Me; for John baptized with water, but you will be baptized with the Holy Spirit not many days from now." Acts 1:4-5 HCSB

"But you will receive power when the Holy Spirit has come upon you, and you will be My witnesses in Jerusalem, in all Judea and Samaria, and to the ends of the earth." Acts 1:8 HCSB

The overflowing presence of the Holy Spirit in the lives of Jesus' followers would empower their testimony of Jesus — the Lord and Messiah — that was to be shared with the entire world.

Have you been baptized *with* the Holy Spirit?

What is *your* Biblical understanding (not religious tradition or human viewpoint) about the Holy Spirit?

Are you seeking to be filled with the Holy Spirit, as Jesus' followers were (Acts chapter 2)?

"Which one of you fathers would give your hungry child a snake if the child asked for a fish? Which one of you would give your child a scorpion if the child asked for an egg? As bad as you are, you still know how to give good gifts to your children. But your heavenly Father is even more ready to give the Holy Spirit to anyone who asks." Luke 11:11-13 CEV

"I assure you: The one who believes in Me will also do the works that I do. And he will do even greater works than these, because I am going to the Father." John 14:12 HCSB

Are you thirsty for more of God's presence in your life?

Could it be said that you zealously ask for and seek God's presence and involvement in your life?

What are the "works" that Jesus did? As a believer and follower of Jesus, are you available to do similar "works" in Jesus' name, as He wills?

"I, Jesus, have sent my angel to give you this testimony for the churches. I am the Root and the Offspring of David, and the bright Morning Star." The Spirit and the bride say, "Come!" And let the one who hears say, "Come!" Let the one who is thirsty come; and let the one who wishes take the free gift of the water of life. Revelation 22:16-17 NIV

Then the one sitting on the throne said: I am making everything new. Write down what I have said. My words are true and can be trusted. Everything is finished! I am Alpha and Omega, the beginning and the end. I will freely give water from the life-giving fountain to everyone who is thirsty. All who win the victory will be given these blessings. I will be their God, and they will be my people. Revelation 21:5-7 CEV

How have you been affected by the examples of these women who encountered Jesus?

Write a summary of what you have learned about Jesus through this personal journey called *Portrait of a Woman and Jesus.*

What have you learned about yourself?

How has this journey changed you?

Do you feel boldly empowered to join Jesus' followers on the mission to share the wonderful news of the eternal peace we have with God through Jesus?

"I am not praying just for these followers. I am also praying for everyone else who will have faith because of what my followers will say about me." John 17:20 CEV

What words of truth spoken by Jesus have impacted you most?

Are you more encouraged to share those words with others?

Jesus' believers were empowered to tell others about the good news of Jesus, but also showed by their actions that they had been transformed by the Holy Spirit. Do others see the impact of Jesus' grace in your life?

How does Jesus' love translate to your life?

"But I am giving you a new command. You must love each other, just as I have loved you. If you love each other, everyone will know that you are my disciples." John 13:34-35 CEV

"This is what I say to all who will listen to me: Love your enemies, and be good to everyone who hates you. Ask God to bless anyone who curses you, and pray for everyone who is cruel to you." Luke 6:27-28 CEV

"Make your light shine, so that others will see the good that you do and will praise your Father in heaven." Matthew 5:16 CEV

Can you visualize standing face-to-face with Jesus?

How deeply do you yearn or long for that time?

What feelings wash over you by the notion of facing Jesus?

I pray that by reading about the women featured in this book, you are encouraged to bring your forgiven, redeemed, restored and rested heart and stand confidently before Your Savior and Friend. He loves you so much that He did whatever was necessary — even giving His life — for you to spend eternity in all its fullness with the Creator and Eternal God. May the compelling stories of these witnesses to Jesus' life, death and resurrection inspire you with a renewed passion to follow Him face-to-face and heart-to-heart the rest of your days!

As for me, the author: One day I long to look deeply into Jesus' eyes and bask in the glow of His glorious presence. Yes, I imagine that I will first kneel, bowing in gratitude and awe at finally knowing the full reality of my Savior and Redeemer. Then I hope Jesus asks me to dance with Him in a joyful celebration of victory and freedom!

Your Encounter With Jesus

Jesus, what are You trying to teach me through the example of Your faithful follower, Mary Magdalene? Write what you are hearing Him say to you.

- Is Jesus asking, **"Who is it you are looking for?"**

- Is He calling *your* name?

My Prayer For You

Jesus, will You reveal Yourself to a greater degree to this dear woman. Lift any fog that clouds her vision and open her eyes to see YOU! Clearly show Yourself and let her experience Your unconditional love toward her. Remind her of Your goodness and willingness to die for her sins so that she may live throughout eternity in Your presence. Please help her to see that she is cherished and delighted in and that You came to earth to restore her relationship with God that was created and intended from the beginning.

Give this woman hope for the time when she will see You face-to-face and experience Your full glory. Answer all of her questions about who You are, laying to rest any lingering doubts, incomplete images or interpretations of who You truly are. May she experience the same power that raised the Son of God from the dead. Help her to know how precious You are and let her see how precious she is in Your eyes. Fill her with the Holy Spirit so that she will boldly proclaim the truth of who You are by sharing the personal story of her relationship with You. Thank You, Jesus! In Your name, I humbly and gratefully pray! Amen!

Your Prayer

Thoughts Regarding Your Journey Experience

EPILOGUE

PORTRAIT OF YOUR ENCOUNTER WITH JESUS

The Biblical stories about the various encounters women had with Jesus provide a more complete understanding of who Jesus is and His purpose for coming to earth. Essentially, Jesus lived, died and was resurrected to save, restore and give life to all humanity. Just as with the women of the Bible, Jesus is pursuing *you* out of the crowd. He understands *your* background and situation, and He knows *your* name. He desires to comfort *you* in times of stress and uncertainty. He has eagerly forgiven, redeemed and saved *you*! Jesus will never give up on *you*. And dear woman, Jesus will not abandon *you* — He has unlimited patience, compassion and empathy. He longs to be *your* friend (John 15:15) and share all aspects of *your* life — *your* ups, downs, challenges and joys.

Are you convinced?

Have your questions regarding God's opinion of you been answered?

What wonderful truth to know that we, too, can have a relationship with the Eternal God of the universe! We are unconditionally loved! Jesus' sacrificial act on the cross reconciled us to our heavenly Father, and those who accept His love will share eternity with Him. We may not see Jesus in the flesh as these women did, but through the Holy Spirit, we have Jesus living in us, and we can experience Him in a variety of ways that He chooses to reveal to us. Because Jesus Christ is the same yesterday and today and forever (Hebrews 13:8), we know He desires to relate to us personally, just as He did with the women He met while on this earth. The Holy Spirit gives us glimpses into His everlasting love for us and ministers to us, even during those times when we don't see clearly.

Do you truly believe that?

"COME TO ME"

Jesus said, **"Come to Me"** (Matthew 11:28). Therefore, you can approach Him with courage, confidence and freedom, having faith that He is who He says He is. There may be times when God seems silent or distant, but just as the mother respectfully persisted in her pleas, be encouraged to keep moving forward toward Him, trusting in His faithfulness, while waiting for His timing to respond. Continue to be open-hearted and ready to hear His voice when He calls.

"Come near to God, and he will come near to you." James 4:8 NIV

Jesus will wait for you to come to Him. His unconditional love allows humans the free will to choose to accept, surrender and trust in Him. He will always be there, inviting and pursuing you. But He will wait. He will not force Himself on you, but gives you the freedom to choose to believe and trust in Him.

How is Jesus waiting for you? What area of your life is He waiting for you to surrender into His capable hands?

"Ask, Seek, Knock"

We have seen examples of women who were compelled and determined to seek Jesus out. Some had physical needs, some spiritual needs, and some were drawn to His message of hope. Their examples are intended to encourage *you* to diligently seek Jesus — to pursue Him, surrender to Him, listen to Him and learn from Him. Ask Him to complete you, to answer your questions, allay your doubts and fill in any gaps in your understanding of who He is. He promises that He will respond, so be confident and persistent in your pursuit of Him.

> ***"For everyone who asks receives; the one who seeks finds; and to the one who knocks, the door will be opened."*** Luke 11:10 NIV

Do you fear those times when Jesus looks into your darkest places in your life and heart? Do you doubt that you are worthy to be loved by Him? Surrender your fears. Believe that God's nature is perfectly good and that He always has your best interests at heart. Trust that He is THE solution to your problems. He is the *only One* who can give you living water to quench the thirst of your heart and the only One who knows the truth of what God's will is for your life.

> *"For I know the plans I have for you," declares the LORD, "plans to prosper you and not to harm you, plans to give you hope and a future. Then you will call upon me and come and pray to me, and I will listen to you. You will seek me and find me when you seek me with all your heart."* Jeremiah 29:11-13 NIV

Because God loves you and desires to have an intimate and eternal relationship with you, *expect* to have an encounter with Him. In fact, as you continue to come to Him and pursue Him, expect *many* encounters with Him. As you earnestly seek and become aware of God's presence in your life, you will experience Him in ways that touch your unique heart, providing personal stories to share with others of how you have experienced God's goodness.

What unanswered questions and unresolved issues do you lay at Jesus' feet?

"I Will Be With You"

Jesus will not leave you alone or forsake you (Hebrews 13:5). He is actively seeking *you* and desires for you to experience the many roles He plays in your life. Just as Psalm 103:3-5 describes, you may experience the Lord as God who heals, God who forgives, God who redeems, God who crowns with love and righteousness, God who satisfies your desires and God who restores. Maybe you will experience Him as God who dances, God who comforts and God who counsels. During your journey with Jesus you will experience Him through a variety of ways that will be personal to *you*.

Maybe your encounter with Jesus will come from one of His words in Scripture, from a word of encouragement from one of His followers, or through the lyrics of a song. Your encounter may come in the form of an answer to prayer or an open door that speaks of God's goodness and personal involvement in your life. A direct word spoken, a vision or a miraculous delivery could be other ways that you might experience God's intervention in your life. Most likely you will be surprised and awed at how God chose to interact and respond to you.

The portrait of your encounter will capture the moment when Jesus looked through your eyes and into the depths of your heart, saw a need or desire and then responded. Maybe you are lonely, grieving or need a rescue or release from guilt. Only God understands your deepest thoughts, desires and needs that are expressed in your heart. When He answers, you will know you have intimately encountered Him. Each of your portraits will show how God revealed Himself personally because He desires for you to experience His unlimited love.

An encounter with Jesus brings joy and a deep sense of peace, with the awareness He has answered one of your central identity questions: Do you love me? Am I beautiful in Your eyes? Do I have value? Do I have a significant purpose? Am I safe? The Holy Spirit will help you to perceive the encounter with Jesus to be genuine, as only He understands the deepest thoughts, desires and needs that are expressed in your heart.

Have you been reassured that Jesus is always with you?

"Remember"

The women and men who were privileged to interact with Jesus had a definitive encounter to recall. They continued to cherish what they had seen, heard and experienced. Though Jesus was gone, what remained was the recollection of the encounter. No one could take away their story and what it meant to them personally.

As you experience God, it is helpful to chronicle your various portraits so you will remember the details of each encounter. How did God reveal Himself to you? What was it about the encounter that specifically addressed the need or desire of your heart? Why was it personal to you? How did God show His goodness and kindness toward you?

Ask the Holy Spirit to bring to remembrance past events in your life that you might have dismissed as "coincidence." As you periodically review your journal, you will see how God's hand has faithfully been on your life, confirming that His love for you is consistent and His timing is perfect. These personal encounters deepen your relationship with God and your heart overflows with praise, adoration and worship for your indescribably amazing God.

During periods of your life when facing trials or when you feel your faith is flagging, it is helpful to review the journal and bring into remembrance God's faithfulness toward you. Reading the accounts of previous encounters with Jesus will remind you that God has always been with you. Be encouraged to know His love will be apparent again, as you wait for His response.

Do you document when and how you experience God?

"Life To The Full"

As we wait for the time when we will see Jesus face-to-face in the kingdom of God, He intends that we live to the fullest in His kingdom on earth.

"I have come that they may have life and have it in abundance." John 10:10 HCSB

"Your kingdom come. Your will be done on earth as it is in heaven." Matthew 6:10 HCSB

What aspects of a full life, as God originally intended, do you desire? What is His will for your life now? What are the benefits of knowing Jesus, the Lord? Psalm 103:3-5 provides a picture of what an abundant life in Jesus looks like, partially on earth and fully in heaven.

In Jesus, you can walk a life of forgiveness — released from oppression of sin, being transformed by His grace. In Jesus, you have the promise of healing — from physical disease (if not now, in eternity) and from emotional scars. In Jesus, you no longer have shame, condemnation, feelings of ugliness or filthiness, but can experience restoration, reconciliation and wholeness. You have a new lease on life, new energy and joyfulness.

Jesus "crowns you with love and compassion," and He restores your soul and worthiness in His eyes. Because He "redeems you from the pit," you can live with thankfulness for your redemption and with empathy for others as they struggle. He gives you the ability to love others the way you have been loved.

An abundant life is possible through Jesus who "satisfies your desires so that your youth is renewed like the eagle's." You can be confident that God knows you, loves you and is personally concerned with your physical and eternal well-being. His blessings flow from His goodness and faithfulness.

How have you encountered Jesus who desires to give you a life of abundance?

"GO INTO ALL THE WORLD"

Those who encountered Jesus said, "*As for us, we cannot help speaking about what we have seen and heard*" (Acts 4:20 NIV), even when the message about Jesus was opposed. Many risked their lives to attest to the truth of who Jesus was and why He came to earth — the good news of the kingdom of God. I would imagine that those who were blessed with a direct interaction with Jesus shared their stories with family members, neighbors and all who were willing to listen. With the Holy Spirit living in them and compelling them to boldly speak, the message about Jesus' life, death and resurrection spread like a wildfire throughout the region and into the world.

As you encounter Jesus and experience the numerous characteristics of God, one of the natural outcomes is a willingness to share the personal stories of God's goodness in your life. Another response to experiencing God is serving those in need, while sharing Jesus' love. As your relationship with Jesus grows by spending time with Him in prayer and seeking His words of truth, your heart for others will begin to beat in unison with His. You will desire to bring God's reconciliation to every person you meet. Jesus' love for the world will become your love for the world, and He will send you to bring His desire for restoration and wholeness to others.

Are you more compelled than ever to tell others, "Come and see my Jesus!"?

MY PRAYER FOR YOU

My Father in heaven, as the reader and I come to the end of our journey together, I thank You for giving me the opportunity to share these words with her. I have no doubt that You have touched the deepest part of her heart with Your love. I trust she has experienced Your genuine gaze on her face and feels Your encompassing comfort, peace and joy. Lord, I ask that she become increasingly aware of Your continual pursuit of her and that she finds it natural to respond to Your presence. As she seeks and asks, please show up in such a powerful and tangible way that she can no longer question Your delight in her.

Jesus, will You surprise her with many encounters as she looks expectantly for You to show up in her life? Give her an increasing understanding of the sacrifice You paid on her behalf so she can spend eternity with You. Father, thank You for making this possible by sending Your Son, Your only Son, to reveal and reconcile Yourself to her. Compel and encourage her to share this wonderful news and stories of her encounters with all whom she comes into contact. In Jesus' name, again I humbly and gratefully pray. Amen!

But these are written so that you may believe Jesus is the Messiah, the Son of God, and by believing you may have life in His name. John 20:31 HCSB

Final Thoughts Regarding Your Journey Experience

PORTRAIT OF MY ENCOUNTER WITH JESUS

A couple of my closest friends have encouraged me to share my encounter with Jesus from which the vision of the book *Portrait of a Woman and Jesus* was conceived. Not only did this particular encounter impact me in an indescribably intimate way, but because of the manner in which the encounter was presented, it became the foundation for the purpose and style of the book.

In childhood, I was introduced to God — a heavenly Father who sent His Son to die for the sins of the world. Although I was a "good girl," at a young age I became acutely aware of my imperfections and recognized the need for a Savior — Jesus — to reconcile me to a perfect and holy God. I knew that of myself, I would never be "good enough" to earn eternal life and therefore, accepted Jesus as my Savior, was baptized and gratefully received the Holy Spirit.

For many years, my spiritual journey was clouded by performance-based theology which took the focus off an intimate relationship with Jesus. After experiencing a dead-end exposure to religious legalism, I had a dramatic awakening which forced me to reevaluate my spiritual foundation. Challenged out of my "comfort zone," I sought a fresh start with Jesus. Slowly I began to become acquainted with Jesus in a new way, primarily through the Biblical stories of the encounters He had with women. My eyes were opened to see the unconditional and grace-filled love of my heavenly Father and His Son. I began to understand God's heart for all people and His desire for us to live fully and freely through and in Jesus, the fulfillment of the Law — the Messiah.

Jesus became the center of my world. No longer was I bound by human religion — with its rules, regulations and denominational theology. Everything in my life began to be filtered through my growing relationship with Jesus and as I experienced who He is to me and all humanity.

It was during this season of life that I also began exploring the core areas of a woman's identity, as they relate to a feminine heart. I had experienced decades of life, played a variety of women's roles and listened to numerous women's stories, giving me an understanding of the struggles and challenges universally experienced by women. As I observed how Jesus related to women, I was convinced that Jesus still desires to relate to every woman in a personal, relevant and intimate way.

During this period of reawakening, my relationship with God went from my head and into my heart. One night a vision came to mind that was undeniably from God. Though it played out like a dream, I was conscious enough to understand the personal nature of the vision and tearfully documented the details in my journal. Because this vision was used as the structure for the book, I will present it in the same way as the portraits in my book *Portrait of a Woman and Jesus*. In this case, though, the thoughts and feelings are real — not imagined — because they happened within the context of *my* encounter with Jesus.

This is *my* portrait of when Jesus spoke to me. My life has never been the same. I share it only to offer encouragement that Jesus is pursuing *you* and desires to have an intimate relationship with *you*. I hope you are blessed by this last portrait.

The Woman Who Was Chosen

The Scene

One would think that every woman in the Kingdom would have wanted to be at the Celebration Ball. The buzz of excitement in the ballroom was electric. A throng of people had gathered in anticipation of seeing the Prince and each wore their finest gowns and robes. The leaders of the Kingdom were vying for a position close to His Highness, and the ladies of the court jostled to catch His eye. One quiet and plain-looking woman was grateful for the invitation to the Ball, but felt as though she did not belong. More comfortable away from the limelight, she observed the activity from afar. In the eyes of the "important" people in attendance, she was nameless, without pedigree or position — present, but invisible.

This young lady enjoyed living in the Kingdom. She always felt secure under the watchful, yet distant care of the Father of the Prince. Today, even though she was in attendance, she did not feel that she was truly included. As she stood by one of the supporting pillars of the ballroom and in the shadows, her mind wandered to familiar places in the countryside where she felt free and safe to explore.

Occasionally, she would glance in the direction of the Prince, wondering what He was saying to those around Him. As she compared her simple blue dress with the other brightly adorned gowns worn by confident and engaging women, her feelings of insignificance grew into sadness. She was too shy to move toward Him and join those gathered around Him. What would she say if He ever spoke to her? No, it wasn't possible He would ever notice her and she looked away, unaware of the movement around her.

Had she kept her eyes on the Prince, she would have noticed His gaze was suddenly centered toward the back of the ballroom. Conversation subsided as those around Him looked with curiosity toward the direction of His focus. Slowly, yet with a determined stride, the Prince moved through the crowd, each person stepping aside to clear a path as He approached.

What had caught the attention of the Prince in such an intentional way? It was now clear He was focused on a person — but who was the focal point of the Prince? The ballroom became uncommonly silent, bringing the lady back to an awareness of her surroundings. She casually looked up, and standing before her, with eyes fixed on her face, was the Prince, Beloved Son of His Father! And He was extending His right hand toward her!

He Looked Into Her Heart

Standing before the Prince was one of His loyal subjects, wearing an expression of disbelief on her face. She habitually and momentarily glanced downward, and then looked up as a guarded smile began to form. The Prince had seen this woman on numerous occasions, though she was unaware she was known by Him. He perceived a heart genuinely yearning to be obedient to the Master and His rules for the Kingdom. This woman wanted to live peaceably with all and had told others the Father of the Kingdom was good and that He knew what was best for all. The Prince also looked into her humble heart which felt unworthy to meet the Father of the Kingdom or His Beloved Son. She was convinced she had nothing of human value or significance to offer to her Lord.

Looking through her blue eyes and into her unpretentious heart, He stepped closer, offered His hand and posed the question that changed her world.

His Response

"Will you dance with Me?"

Was the Prince actually asking *her* to dance with *Him*? She gasped with astonishment and could not seem to find her voice to respond. How did He know she loved to dance? Stretching His hand closer toward her, He asked again, "Will you dance with Me?" Still speechless, she hesitantly lifted up her chin toward Him, looked into His eyes, straightened her shoulders and gracefully placed her hand into His. Together, hand-in-hand and face-to-face, the Prince and His chosen lady slowly walked to the center of the ballroom, and then they danced . . . and danced . . . and danced.

The Outcome

While waltzing around the ballroom as the crowd quietly watched, time seemed to stand still. Though it felt like a dream (but she knew it wasn't because her heart was beating wildly), this quiet woman in the nondescript blue dress cherished every moment of this special encounter. After the Ball was over, she would giggle to herself, remembering the day the Prince had chosen *her* to dance with Him.

In some ways, life for this woman was the same after her momentous dance. Her status and position did not change, though the townspeople were more curious and intrigued by her. The biggest difference was that she no longer felt invisible, insignificant or plain in comparison to others. She lived as before, but with the awareness that she was seen, known and valued in the eyes of the Prince. Her heart longed for the day when she would dance with Him again in His heavenly Kingdom.

This grateful lady lived out the rest of her days recounting the story of her encounter with Jesus, her Prince, the Beloved Son of the Father. She would tell of the goodness of the Prince who valued her so much that He would invite her to dance with Him. She would share with others how the Prince includes all individuals in His Kingdom, without exception. Each person is significant, beautiful in His eyes and loved for who they uniquely are by the Prince and His Father. All are invited to participate as ambassadors in adventures of significance for their Kingdom.

Through His Spirit living in this chosen lady, she regularly called to remembrance the encounter she had with the Prince. It was her story and no one could take it away from her. With time, her relationship with the Prince deepened, and her heart learned to beat in unison with His. To all who were willing to listen to her story, she would say, "Come and hear about *my* Jesus, the Prince who asked me to dance eternally with Him!"

About The Author

Barbara Quillen Egbert credits her life experiences — in the roles of wife, mother, published author, educator, camp director and ministry leader — as the foundation to her interest in and understanding of women's identity issues as they relate to God's original intent for their lives.

One of her most fulfilling roles was that of camp director of the SEP Camp in Minnesota where she was lovingly nicknamed "Momma Egbert." It was during her involvement at the camp that she met the actor who portrayed Jesus in the *Matthew* film. Through Bruce Marchiano's portrayal and personal testimony, the author was given a glimpse of the zealous love Jesus has for each of God's children, inspiring her quest to relate heart-to-heart with Him.

Due to the insights gained through her spiritual journey, the author can confidently state that a woman's identity issues are primarily addressed through an intimate relationship with Jesus. Her interest in art combined with a personal encounter with Jesus provided the inspiration for the concept of the book — verbally and artistically capturing a portrait of a woman's encounter with Jesus.

As a ministry leader, she readily shares her journey of experiencing God and encourages others to seek their own personal relationship with Jesus. Her greatest joy is when others experience the love, restoration and peace found only in Him.

Born in Colorado, Barb has also lived in Iowa and Texas and now resides in California with her husband. She is blessed with three grown children and enjoys riding her cruiser bike along the beach, dancing, sailing, playing harp, tutoring young learners and walking through life with her friends. She loves exploring the coast of California in search of scenic places to write and experience God and His beautiful creation.

About The Artist

Wilson Jay Ong grew up in the San Francisco Bay Area and received a BFA from Brigham Young University and afterward attended the Art Students' League. In addition to being a professional artist and illustrator since 1983, Wilson has taught art, presented workshops and exhibited his work nationally. He and his family currently live in Corning, New York.

> *"Concerning this project, I consider it a tremendous challenge and privilege to paint scenes from the life of the Savior. Nevertheless, it has been exciting to imagine, in particular, the tenderness with which He cared for the women in His life and others He came in contact with during His ministry."* — Wilson Jay Ong